RETREATS

IN

EVERYDAY

LIFE

A HANDBOOK
FOR A MONTH OF
INDIVIDUALLY
GUIDED PRAYER

William V. Thompson

First Published by Open House Publications

Second Edition 2005

ISBN 0-9551859-0-4

Printed and bound by Antony Rowe Ltd, Eastbourne

Open House
Publications

Contents

Acknowledgement

My thanks are due to those who have helped in the journey that has led to the development of this book which has arisen from the experience of Months of Individually Guided Prayer in Everyday Life held in the Yeovil area of Somerset.

Firstly, I am indebted to Father Dermot Mansfield S.J., who initially introduced me to the dynamic of such Months of Individually Guided Prayer and on whose work much of the following is based. Equally I recall with much gratitude to God, the three months that I spent in St. Beuno's in the Autumn of 1990, exploring Ignatian Spirituality and those who kindly welcomed me into that community of faith.

This material has been worked with for some years with a group of my friends from the Yeovil Baptist Church and the Town Centre Churches Ecumenical Partnership who have shared with me in directing these Months of Individually Guided Prayer in Everyday Life. I want to acknowledge my deep debt of gratitude to them for their patience and love in this special experience of faith. So to Heather Andrews, Barbara Carpenter, Chris Redman, Heather Voizey and many others who have shared the journey along the way, my sincere thanks. I am also tremendously indebted to Michael Lee of Open House Publications in Bath for his generous help and expertise in helping me progress this piece of work to publication.

William V. Thompson

Foreword

Both within the church and among those who have nothing to do with institutional religion, there is an increasing interest in spirituality. So much so that a book recently published has the title "Spiritual Revolution". People, many of them young, are searching for meaning in life. A retreat (a strange term for what is often an advance, a life-changing experience), is an opportunity to get in touch with our real selves, to examine where we are on our journey in life and the route for the future. As Will Thompson tells us in this book, not everyone has the inclination or the opportunity to go away to a retreat house for this. It can be done at home while carrying on with one's daily tasks. Doing it this way, it is amazing how the prayer exercises so often fit into what is happening currently in our lives.

This book provides an excellent description of a retreat in daily life. More than that, it gives all that is necessary for planning such a retreat. It is a distillation of Will Thompson's long and wide experience of setting up and giving these retreats. It is practical and detailed. As I read the proofs, such was my excited interest that I longed to make copious notes but realised thankfully that the book itself will be available shortly. May it be the source of much blessing to many who wish to advance on their spiritual journey and to those who accompany them.

The Rt. Revd. Graham Chadwick

Salisbury
Christmas 2004

Preface

To the

Second Edition

This Second Edition of A Handbook for a Month of Individually Guided Prayer is in a completely new format.

I have rearranged the order of the contents to reflect our experience of the use of the material and the comments of those who used the old edition. This edition also contains some new material that we have felt would be helpful for those contemplating this ministry of retreats in everyday life.

I hope that this new edition will be of benefit to those using it.

I would want to emphasise the imperative of flexibility. This handbook represents our experience and we are constantly adapting and reordering our own practice year by year depending on those who come on our Months and Weeks of Individually Guided Prayer, I commend that to anyone who may use this book. Allow the Lord to lead you, as we believe the Lord leads us and our retreatants.

The Lord be with you.

William V. Thompson

Autumn 2004

Using the Material of this Handbook:

The material in this Handbook is divided into four sections.

Section One is an introduction to the dynamics of a Month of Individually Guided Prayer.

Section Two contains notes about the planning of the Month of Individually Guided Prayer with details about the shape and timing of sessions and the meetings of those leading the retreat. Also included in this Section are a series of Scripture Passages that may be used during the retreat.

Section Three contains material that makes up the initial folder that is given to the retreatant during the opening session. The retreatant's folder is an important starting point for the person beginning a Month of Individually Guided Prayer and it needs to be of a high quality and well presented, with the retreatant's name on the front cover.

This gives to the retreatant a sense of belonging and the quality of the folder equally speaks of the value and importance of the retreat journey upon which the retreatant is about to embark.

The folder needs to contain a number of blank sheets of paper for the retreatants to use for their own Review of Prayer, or Prayer Journal, should they so wish.

Section Four is the material that is added to the retreatant's folder at the end of the retreat, mention of these are made during details of the Closing Session.

The piece entitled "Scriptures to Pray with" is given as an example. We suggest that three Scriptures are included for each week for a period of three months following the end of the retreat. These Scriptures could well be chosen relating to the season of the Christian year, using the Lectionary or Scriptures of your own choice.

Experience has shown that after a Month of Individually Guided Prayer the retreatant has not only begun to get used to a pattern of daily prayer, but desires guidance in continuing the discipline of the retreat and this piece seeks to provide the necessary material to meet such desire.

Section Four contains a collection of non-scriptural material that we have found useful for prayer and meditation during our retreats.

For some, a written evaluation sheet is an important and useful part of a retreat. We, however have come to favour an oral evaluation, in the first place with the Prayer Guide, at the end of the retreat. If the retreatant, after reflection on their experience, wishes to write some evaluation then we welcome such feedback.

A Note on Flexibility

At the heart of the Spiritual Exercises of Ignatius Loyola lies a basic reminder to the one giving the Exercises, that the director needs always to be aware of the needs of the retreatant and therefore has to be flexible in both planning and giving the retreat.

> Sp.Ex. 18   *"The Spiritual Exercises must be*
> *adapted to the condition of the one who*
> *is to engage in them, that is their age,*
> *education, and talent."*

The pages of this handbook relate to a **Month of Individually Guided Prayer in Everyday Life** and the imperative of flexibility that we find in the Spiritual Exercises applies to such retreats in everyday life. Without too much difficulty the pattern for a Month of Individually Guided Prayer can easily be adapted to either

A Week of Guided Prayer - with a daily pattern of meetings with the retreatants and their prayer guides over the time span of seven days,

or

giving the retreat over a period of **two or more weeks**, again with the frequency of meeting between retreatant and prayer guided adjusted to suit the length of time for the whole retreat.

The important instruction for anyone planning such a retreat in everyday life is that the imperative to flexibility is held constantly in mind, namely suiting the retreat to the retreatant, in order that the Lord may be able to work in and through the experience of the retreat to the benefit of the retreatant and their spiritual journey and growth.

SECTION

Introducing the dynamics of a Month of Individually Guided Prayer

ONE

A Month of Individually Guided Prayer

Not everyone has the inclination or the opportunity to go away on a retreat, whether for three or thirty days. Responsibilities at home, work, or in the Church, quite apart from the financial considerations, can often make it impossible for some to even consider the possibility of a retreat away from home in a Retreat Centre. Equally, fear and a lack of confidence can play their part in fighting shy of the whole idea of making a retreat:

> "That's not for me, and anyway my prayer
> life is in a mess, in fact even non-existent
> and anyway I'm not that high powered."

This kind of thinking can make people run a mile from the idea of drawing near to God in a special way in a retreat setting. Despite these fears, many people have a desire to grow in their own inner journey with the Lord and to explore new possibilities in their life, ministry and service of the Kingdom. A Month of Individually Guided Prayer is a wonderful way of making an individually guided retreat in the midst of our everyday lives.

First of all it is **individually guided**; so this kind of a retreat is tailor made for where an individual is in their own spiritual journey. There is no question of being "good enough". All that is needed is a desire to draw near to God and an openness and generosity of spirit to be led by the Spirit in our journey of prayer with the Lord.

The original inspiration for these times of Directed Prayer in Everyday Life came from Father John Veltri SJ. of Loyola House at Guelph in Canada, where this format was used as Weeks of Guided Prayer. These were further developed in Dublin by Father Dermot Mansfield SJ. and others and then by centres like St. Beuno's in North Wales. The Month of Guided Prayer gives more time to explore the dynamic of the Spirit's working in our lives and to notice the movements in our prayers, as well as getting accustomed to the discipline of listening prayer and the reviewing of that prayer. In this journey with the Lord we touch the depths of the mystery that we know as life, as God meets us in His love, in His own way and in His own time. It is this element of time that the Month of Guided Prayer gives to a retreatant.

Perhaps the most important element of this whole retreat experience is its **simplicity** - and we try to preserve that characteristic in everything that we do. Above all, the simple beauty of such a retreat is that **it works.** It is a profoundly moving experience of being directed by God and of sharing that journey with another person who travels along with the retreatant.

The person accompanying the retreatant we call their "Spiritual Director", but we need always to remember that the real director of the retreat is the Holy Spirit. The retreat director is there to share this unique journey with the retreatant, noticing the direction that God may be leading their companion. For the retreat director this is truly "holy ground" and there is no greater privilege than to share in such a journey with another pilgrim.

The format of the retreat is based on a commitment of making half an hour of prayer with Scripture each day, followed by a time of reviewing the prayer. All this is done at home. So we are asking the retreatant to make a maximum commitment of less than one hour a day. In addition, the retreatant is invited to meet with his/her spiritual director twice each week for up to half an hour to explore the journey together. This meeting takes place at an agreed centre for the Month. The retreat as a whole starts with one group session on the first day and ends with another whole group session on the last day of the retreat.

The choice of centre is important and it may be possible to hold the retreat in a home with an adequate number of rooms. Such a homely base helps to emphasise the everyday nature of this kind of retreat. There needs to be a room large enough for all to meet in, facilities for refreshments, and individual rooms for direction sessions during the retreat with a reasonable degree of privacy.

A church may have suitable rooms that are welcoming and comfortable, that offers privacy and has separate facilities for refreshments. Which ever meeting place is chosen, consideration needs to be given to car parking arrangements and the need for privacy in the direction sessions.

The participants come from all walks of life and at all stages of spiritual experience. The special part of the Month of Guided Prayer is that it is individually guided, matching the needs of each individual and their experience at the time of the retreat, as God is allowed to speak through the Scriptures *(Hebrews 4; 12f)* and their own experience. Each retreatant needs to come with an open and generous heart and a desire to deepen their own life of prayer, to learn how to pray with Scripture and to explore the mystery of God's love in their life and their world.

The Spiritual Directors, or Prayer Guides as they are sometimes called, seek to facilitate the journey into that deeper experience of love and freedom in the Lord, as each participant encounters Him through the Word of God.

It is always the director's primary aim not to get in the way of the spiritual journey of the retreatant. It is God who leads and directs each retreatant through the Month of Individually Guided Prayer. The directors are there to share the journey and help the traveller to notice the movements of God's grace and love along the way, listening with an open ear as well as an open heart to the voice of God whose journey we share together as pilgrims on the way of faith. The director will need to seek to be like a balance at equilibrium, to use Ignatius' picture, so that they can discern the movements, nudges and call of God as the journey progresses.

> *Sp. Ex. 15*   *"Therefore, the director of the Exercises, as a balance at equilibrium, without leaning to one side or the other, should permit the Creator to deal directly with the creature, and the creature directly with the Creator and Lord."*

Planning the Month of

Individually Guided Prayer

Choosing the Prayer Team

The Spiritual Director or Prayer Guide

It is a tremendous privilege to be involved in sharing another's journey with the Lord, whether in a retreat in Everyday Life or in a closed retreat. A spiritual director or prayer guide needs first of all to be conscious of God's call upon their own life and own a sense of the grace that invites sinners to such service.

The prayer guide needs to be there for the retreatant in love and with a generous heart, knowing that they too are the recipients of God's unbounded love. The prayer guide will need to listen above all else with ear and heart. Young Solomon prayed that God would give him a "heart with skill to listen", in order that he might be able to discern the will of God for his people. *(1 Kings 3; 9)* Such a listening ministry is about companionship and sharing in the retreatant's journey and allowing them to explore God's will and purpose in their lives. It is always their journey that is important and not that of the prayer guide.

The prayer guide needs to be true to themselves and to their companion as they travel together in the grace and love of God. It is not their place to dictate or rule over the retreatant on their journey. It is not for them to seek to solve problems or remove pain along the way. Rather, it is to allow the Lord to work with the retreatant in His own time in His own way, always bearing in mind that the retreat is not an end in itself but a part of the journey with the ever present Lord.

During his Presidential Address to the Baptist Union of Great Britain Assembly in Cardiff in 2003, The Revd. John Rackley quoted the following from Vincent Donovan on the subject of our missionary task of accompanying others in their search for God.

*"Do not try to call them back
to where they were
and do not call them to where
you are,
as beautiful as that place might
seem to you.*

*You must have the courage to
go with them
to a place that neither you nor
they have ever been before."*

Hosting

It is an invaluable part of the retreat to have a member of
the Prayer Team to act as host for the retreatants, to meet
them on arrival and offer tea/coffee before and after their
time of direction. This time can be of crucial importance as
it is the retreatant's point of arrival and departure. Not
everyone may want to be part of this social interaction, but a
good host will sensitively notice any changes in a
retreatant's pattern, which may indicate movement in their
journey of prayer. This can prove to be a tremendously
valuable ingredient to the whole Month of Guided Prayer.
We have found that retreatants have been really encouraged
and deeply moved by the presence of a good and generous
host.

Meetings and commitment of The Prayer Team

It is vital for the Prayer Team, including the host for the
retreat, to meet together well before the retreat begins, for
prayer and to make the necessary arrangements for the
retreat. Attention needs to be given to publicity, finance,
venue, including the hosting of the retreat and the
composition of the direction groups. Preparation for
directing another in retreat is so important and involves
exploring the question of discernment and listening skills,

text selection and confidentiality, to enable the director to be a true facilitator in the retreat experience.

During the retreat the directors come together three-quarters of an hour before the start of each session, for prayer, encouragement and for sharing, including the reflection on text selection where necessary.

Plan this meeting to be for half an hour, which then allows fifteen minutes to ensure that all will be ready for the arrival of the first retreatants. Experience suggests that some retreatants will arrive early!

Team members take their turn in leading the meeting. Start the meeting with ten minutes of silent prayer. During this time we bring before the Lord, each other as members of the team, the people we are directing and the whole work of the evening.

It is important that the whole team is present for this, both directors and host.

❑ Time is then given to sharing concerns and approaches to such things as the opening interviews, some discussion of text selection, and reflections on how to deal with anger, lack of forgiveness, bereavement, the desire to run, guilt, etc.

❑ It is important to remember to check every so often, and at least after a week or so of the retreat, that the retreatants are happy with the process; i.e. time, place, review, repetition.

❑ The meeting ends with a time of brief prayer and an opportunity to relax together, ready for the ongoing work of the session.

After each session it is useful for the directors to meet, to unwind and share together, bearing in mind the need to retain the absolute confidentiality of the retreatants.

A week or so after the retreat, the Prayer Team needs to meet again for further prayer to evaluate the retreat and to make plans for the future.

If this ministry is ongoing, then the Prayer Team should meet at regular intervals between retreats for prayer, ongoing training and planning.

Supervision

An important element of leading any retreat is the life of the Team of Directors and their mutual support and encouragement. No one embarking on the work of accompanying another in their retreat in everyday life should do so without supervision. Such supervision can be in the form of another person not involved in the retreat itself supervising the Team of Directors, either individually or as a group, or it can be in the form of mutual support, using the regular time of meeting after the direction sessions and a meeting arranged after the end of the retreat.

The Direction Sessions

Each retreatant will come back to the meeting place twice a week, at a time arranged with their director, for up to half an hour. During this time an opportunity will be given for sharing the journey, receiving suggested portions of Scripture and encouragement for the next few days of the retreat.

The prayer material is usually based on Scripture. However other readings, pictures, or activities may be useful to give to particular retreatants. As we will discover in any Directed Retreat in Everyday Life, the time of direction will inevitably involve the unique experiences of life which will naturally surface in the prayer journey of the retreatant.

> *"The word of God is alive and active.*
> *It cuts more keenly than any two-edged*
> *sword, piercing so deeply that it divides*
> *soul and spirit, joints and marrow; it*
> *discriminates among the purposes and*
> *thoughts of the heart. Nothing in all*
> *creation can hide from him; everything*
> *lies bare and exposed to the eyes of*
> *him to whom we must render account."*
> *(Hebrews 4; 12 - 13)*

These words from Hebrews reminds us that in offering Scripture Passages to the retreatant we are offering the "active word of God" in an individual's faith journey.

Beware in giving such treasures, not to say too much about what is given or why it is given, but to allow the retreatant to listen to God's word without prejudice.

Scripture Passages - Resources

First Days

Exodus 33; 18 - 23	*The desire to see God*
Psalm 62; 1 – 8	*Depending on God*
Psalm 63; 1 – 8	*Longing for God*
Psalm 131	*A prayer of humble trust*
Psalm 139; 1 - 18, 23 - 24	*God's complete knowledge*
Isaiah 30; 15, 18	*The Lord is waiting to be merciful*
Isaiah 43; 1 - 7	*God's promise*
Isaiah 46; 3 - 4	*God's care*

Isaiah 49; 14 - 16	The love of God
Isaiah 55; 1 - 3	The food
Jeremiah 1; 4 - 8	Jeremiah's call
Jeremiah 29; 11 - 14	The plan
Hosea 2; 14	The desert and words of love
Zephaniah 3; 15b - 18a	The Lord's gift
Matthew 11; 28 - 30	The Lord's invitation
Mark 10; 46 - 52	Blind Bartimaeus
Luke 1; 26 - 38	The Annunciation
Luke 5; 1 - 11	The call to discipleship
Luke 5; 12 - 16	Jesus' desire to cleanse
Luke 11; 5 - 13	Teach us to pray
Luke 12; 22 - 32	Trust in God
John 1; 35 - 42	The Invitation

Trust

Ecclesiastes 3; 1 - 8	For everything a season
Psalm 46 - 1 - 11	God is our shelter
Psalm 131	Humble Trust
Psalm 139	Knowing and Trusting
Psalm 147; 11	Trust
Isaiah 43 1 - 5	The Promise
Jeremiah 18; 1 - 6	The Potter's House
Jeremiah 29; 11 - 14	The Restorer
Matthew 6; 5 - 15	Prayer of Trust
Matthew 6; 24 - 34	Do not worry
Matthew 11; 28 - 30	The Lord's invitation
Matthew 14; 11 - 22	Feeding 5000
Matthew 14; 22 - 33	Walking on the water
Mark 4; 35 - 41	Calming the storm
Luke 1; 26 - 38	The Annunciation
Luke 6; 17 - 23	Beatitudes
Luke 12; 22 - 32	Trust in God
Luke 21; 1 - 4	The widow's mite
John 12; 24 - 26	Losing and gaining life
John 15; 1 - 8	The vine
Romans 8; 31 - 3	Certainty
Philippians 4; 8 - 13	Confidence in all things

Jesus

Luke 1; 26 - 38	*The Annunciation*
Luke 1; 39 - 45	*The Visit*
Luke 2; 1 - 20	*The Nativity*
Luke 2; 22 - 38	*The Presentation*
Luke 2; 39 - 40, 51 - 52	*The Hidden Life*
Luke 2; 41 - 50	*Jesus in the Temple*
John 1; 1 - 5	*The Word*
John 2; 1 - 12	*Wedding in Cana*
Colossians 1; 15 - 20	*Christ the likeness of God*

Compassion

Luke 2; 22 - 38	*The Presentation*
Luke 4; 16 - 29	*Jesus' manifesto*
Luke 10; 25 - 37	*The Good Samaritan*
Luke 10; 38 - 42	*Martha and Mary*
Luke 15; 11 - 32	*The Loving Father*
Luke 16; 19 - 31	*Dives and Lazarus*
Luke 23; 32 - 43	*Jesus' Prayer*
John 2; 1 - 12	*The Wedding at Cana*
John 4; 1 - 15	*The Well at Sychar*

Jesus and Prayer

Matthew 6; 5 - 6	*Privacy*
Matthew 14; 13 - 32	*A day in the life of Jesus*
Matthew 26; 36 - 46	*Gethsemane*
Mark 1; 35 - 39	*Early and alone in prayer*
Mark 9; 14 - 29	*Boy with an Evil Spirit*
Luke 3; 21 - 22	*The Baptism*
Luke 5; 15 - 16	*Alone in prayer*
Luke 6; 12 - 16	*Prayer before choosing*
Luke 7; 1 - 10	*Centurion's Son*
Luke 9; 18 - 21	*Prayer and challenge*
Luke 9; 28 - 36	*The Transfiguration*
Luke 11; 1 - 4	*The Lord's Prayer*
Luke 11; 5 - 8	*Prayer and Asking*
Luke 11; 9 - 13	*Prayer and Giving*

Luke 22; 39 - 46	*Gethsemane*
John 15; 1 - 17	*The true vine*

Healing

Genesis 32; 22f	*Jacob at Jabok*
Ezekiel 36; 25 - 29	*Sprinkled with clean water*
Hosea 11; 1 - 9	*God's love*
Mark 1; 40 - 45	*The Lord who wants to heal*
Mark 2; 1 - 12	*Jesus heals a Paralysed man*
Mark 5; 21 - 24, 35 - 43	*Jairus' Daughter*
Mark 5; 25 - 34	*A woman's trust*
Mark 7; 31 - 37	*A deaf man*
Mark 8; 22 - 26	*A blind man*
Mark 9; 33 - 37	*Priorities*
Mark 10; 46 - 52	*Bartimaeus*
Luke 5; 12 - 16	*Leprosy*
Luke 5; 17 - 25	*A paralysed man*
Luke 7; 36 - 50	*A sinful woman*
Luke 13; 10 - 17	*A crippled woman*
Luke 15; 11 - 32	*The loving Father*
John 4; 1 - 30	*A Samaritan woman*
John 5; 1 - 18	*The pool of Bethzatha*
John 8; 1 - 11	*Caught in adultery*
John 11; 1 - 44	*Lazarus*
1 Peter 1; 7	*The Refiner's Fire*

Forgive Me

Hosea 11; 1 - 9	*God's love*
Matthew 9; 10 - 13	*Calling sinners*
Luke 7; 36 - 50	*Simon's house*
Luke 15; 11 - 32	*The Loving Father*
Luke 18; 9 - 14	*The Pharisee and the Publican*
Luke 19; 1 - 10	*Zacchaeus*
Luke 23; 33 - 34	*Forgive them*
Luke 23; 39 - 43	*The thief*
John 4; 1 - 30	*A Samaritan woman*
John 8; 1 - 11	*Caught in adultery*
John 21; 15 - 19	*Peter*

Forgiving Others

Matthew 5; 20 - 26	*Anger and reconciliation*
Matthew 5; 43 - 48	*Love for enemies*
Matthew 6; 7 - 15	*The Lord's Prayer*
Matthew 7; 1 - 5	*Judgement*
Luke 23; 33 - 34	*Forgive them*
John 13; 1 - 15	*Washing feet*
1 Corinthians 13; 4 - 13	*Love*

Closing Days

Luke 24; 13 - 35	*The Emmaus Road*
John 13; 1 - 15	*Washing feet*
John 14; 27 - 29	*My peace*
John 21; 15 - 17	*Do you Love me?*
John 21; 18 - 19	*Maturity and discipleship*
Romans 8; 31 - 39	*On my side*
Romans 15; 4 - 6	*Encouragement*
2 Corinthians 4; 6 - 16	*Clay pots*
Galatians 5; 22	*Fruit of the Spirit*
Ephesians 3; 14 - 21	*Paul's Prayer*
Philippians 1; 3 - 11	*Love, knowledge and judgement*
Philippians 4; 4 - 9	*Joy and peace*
Colossians 1; 15 - 20	*The work of Christ*

Evaluation

As the retreat comes to an end it is useful for the retreatant to be invited to reflect upon their journey.

It may be useful to ask the retreatant to spend some time reflecting on the following questions before the retreat ends, so giving time for the retreatant to come back and talk through their experiences.

- ❏ What has God shown me about himself during these days?
- ❏ What has God shown me about myself during the retreat?
- ❏ What has God been inviting me to?
- ❏ How have I responded to the movement of God in me?
- ❏ What fears and resistances have I experienced?
- ❏ What hopes and desires have I felt within me?
- ❏ What implications does this retreat have for my daily life?
- ❏ What do I want to ask God at this time?

The following scripture passages may help at this time:

Jeremiah 29; 11 – 13	*God's Plan*
Isaiah 43; 1	*Called by name*
Isaiah 49; 15 – 16	*Never forgotten*
Mark 8; 34	*Following in the way of the cross*
Mark 5; 33	*What happened?*
1 John 3; 20	*Greater than your heart*

It is important to invite the retreatant to touch into a deep sense of thanksgiving for all that has been given in the time of the retreat and to be conscious of the ongoing generosity of God as the retreat comes to an end.

Discernment

Just a note on the invaluable role we play as directors in walking alongside a fellow pilgrim in their prayer journey through a Month of Individually Guided Prayer.

We are invited to listen with heart and mind to our retreatant's journey. In listening we will need to seek the Lord's help in discerning what the Lord might be saying or doing in the retreatant's life.

When we talk about Discernment we are referring to some guidelines that Ignatius Loyola gives in his Spiritual Exercises. In fact for him, this was the very heart of his own conversion as he reflected on his daydreams following his encounter with a French cannonball that shattered one of his legs during the siege of Pamplona.

In discernment we are looking for the results of a time of prayer and how a retreatant responds and feels in his/her heart. Does the time of prayer leave the retreatant open and at peace with God, or does it leave them closed in on themselves, anxious and despairing?

We are aware that when someone is about the things of the Kingdom, the Evil One is likely to be there in the process seeking to usurp and hinder the work of God. Generally when we are about our own business and little mindful of the Love of God then the Evil One will be content to leave us alone.

So in discernment we need to be listening with our hearts to the movements of the Spirit in our retreatant's life journey. One movement will tend to lead towards what we call "desolation" and another to what we call "consolation".

Both consolation and desolation are felt experiences not to be recognised only by the pleasure or the pain they produce, but what effects they have on our lives, our thinking and our desires.

Consolation

Consolation opens us up and moves us to a greater awareness of God's goodness and love, opening our hearts to the wider call of God in our neighbour and creation. Even though there may be a sense of sadness about our own life and pilgrimage we feel close to God and to others and there is a sense of peace.

In Consolation, we are looking for that felt sense of God's presence, of faith and love. We palpably feel energy coming from God, though often in a quiet way and there is a felt sense of growth in faith, hope and love.

Consolation calls out of the retreatant a positive sense, even an eager desire to action and at the same time a deep inner peace.

Noticing consolation is about discerning the presence of God leading and inviting the retreatant along the pilgrim way.

Desolation

Desolation is completely the opposite of Consolation.

In desolation we notice that the retreatant will be preoccupied with all kinds of difficulties. They will be feeling out of sorts. In desolation the retreatant will be looking at themselves, at their weaknesses and their problems. They will be preoccupied with how well, or more often than not, how badly they are doing. They will be constantly aware of their own point of view and filled with negative feelings about everything.

Notice where their focus is. There will be a perceived lack of energy and they will be depending on themselves and their own knowledge and understanding.

They will still be believing in the Lord, but they will be out of touch with their source of faith and life as their minds are preoccupied with the things of this world and their own understanding.

Desolation indicates that the Evil One is at work. Now there is no need to panic! Scripture is quite clear that the Evil One has been defeated and yet still at work. As directors we need to hear the Lord's words: "Do not be afraid"

In desolation your retreatant may well be very negative and even want to give up. They need to know that the process of desolation is often a tremendous sign of spiritual growth and movement and a scenario to greater things to come. But while in desolation the desert can seem a very barren and painful place indeed, both for the retreatant and for the director who shares the journey with them.

Desolation will turn us back on ourselves and away from the generosity and freedom that God gives. Desolation makes us feel inadequate and alone, as if we are doing all this on our own. There will often be a sense of anger and negativity that may even be turned against the person accompanying the retreatant on their journey. God will seem far away. The problems will be "writ" large.

This is such an important place for the retreatant and the director needs to be prepared to stay with the retreatant, encouraging and supporting them even in their darkest hour. The main rule of thumb is not to actively seek to extricate the retreatant from this desert experience but to trust in God's refining fire in the retreatant's life journey. Pray for your retreatant and beware of your own desire to extricate him/her from this cloud of unknowing, because it is uncomfortable for you as well as for them.

Beware of the desolation that comes as an apparently good thing. Remember that the Evil One is also the Angel of Light and will often present scenarios that at first sight seems nothing but excellent and good. Ask yourself, where is the focus, what is the felt experience of the retreatant and why is this call being given?

Let's look at an example. Your companion is asked to embark on an excellent piece of work very much for the well being of others in the community. But it is already very clear that your retreatant is over busy. We need to discern if this is the Holy Spirit drawing them to this undoubtedly good task, promising his assistance. Or is it the Evil One at work here driving them to take on too much, knowing that all their work will suffer, as will their family life, their life of prayer and ultimately ending up exhausted and broken. We need to be able to discern what is happening here. We need to listen with heart and mind.

How do they feel about saying "No" to this great idea? Maybe on the surface they feel guilty, after all it is a tremendous opportunity for service and witness. But deep down, the idea of saying "No" leaves a sense of lightness and a feeling that this is the right thing to do. There is a deep and real sense of peace in saying "No".

Or is it the other way round? Maybe by saying "Yes" they feel empowered and full of energy, even excitement. To say "No" leaves them feeling empty and saddened and distant from God. In consolation they will feel at peace and even be able to explore the possibility of happily relinquishing other tasks in order to fulfil this one.

In desolation the retreatant may well feel that this is a task too far and yet there is an opportunity for personal advancement and honour to be gained. This will be good for everyone and especially for them and they will worry about any other effects later on, but now let's go for it and all will be well. You will notice the hardness of heart and the forcefulness of the drive and the lack of peace.

A final note.

Not all desolation is necessarily bad. Sometimes we need to be challenged and as it were emptied, in order to be filled anew. Some experiences of desolation lead us to a place where we come in a new way to depend on God and not on ourselves. St. John of the Cross reminds us of the need to be ground out so that space can be given for new gifts and new opportunities of service, but the grinding out process can be both painful and agonising.

So these guidelines in discernment help us to begin to discover which way the Lord may be leading our retreatants along the way.

Opening Session

The aim of the opening session is to meet the retreatants and Prayer Team and to introduce the Month of Individually Guided Prayer. This initial session sets the tone of the retreat and begins to develop the community of prayer. There will be a chance to explore the discipline of the month, including Praying with Scripture, the Review of Prayer, and the practice of Repetition in Prayer. It also provides the opportunity for the retreatants to meet with their directors as part of a smaller direction group and to arrange their own timetable for meetings during the retreat.

Meeting with their director in the direction groups, the retreatants will be given their first set of Scripture passages and have the opportunity to ask further questions and be encouraged as they begin their prayer journey.

We begin as a community who are called together by the Lord and who will be led by Him through the coming weeks of the retreat. By the end of this session, hopefully all the retreatants will feel happy and at ease, ready for their prayer journey, understanding both the time and disciplines needed.

Planning the Opening Session

Timing: Two Hours Max

1. Welcome to everyone
   Brief introduction of retreatants.

2. Introduce direction team including the host, geography of the venue - car parking, entrances, toilets, kitchen and availability of tea/coffee etc.

3. Distribute retreat folders which will include the necessary papers and blank sheets for the Review of Prayer. The folder will be added to at the end of the retreat.

4. **Introduction to the Retreat** [Page 49f]

   Some explanation of the dynamic of an Individually Guided retreat in Everyday Life.

5. An explanation of the month's programme:

   ❑ A daily discipline of 30 minutes of prayer with Scripture plus a time for the Review of Prayer.

   ❑ A meeting with your director twice a week at an agreed time.

   ❑ The ending of the retreat.

6.   The individual meeting with your director.

❑ Time allowed will be 30 minutes, you will need to stay for just as long as required, not necessarily the whole 30 minutes.

❑ Your director, or prayer guide, will be responsible for this time:
  - do not be afraid.
  - silence is good and will be part of the direction time.

❑ Remember:
  - there are no right answers.
  - your prayer journey is your own.
  - you only have to share what you want to.

❑ Talk about how you got on with your prayer time at home:

  - sometimes it will have gone very well indeed.

  - sometimes it will seem that nothing happened at all - that is fine!

  - just be yourself.

  - use your Prayer Journal, which will be your review of prayer and will be a useful resource in recalling to mind the journey of the past few days.

  - plus any help with questions or queries that have arisen along the way and any pointers for the coming days.

❑ You will then receive a new selection of passages of Scripture, or prayer material for the next few days.

7. **Praying with Scripture**   [Page 51f]

Work through the paper, with emphasis on prayer being God centred, the importance of preparing for prayer, centering in prayer and ending the time of prayer.

Suggest the advantage of putting aside one's ordinary disciplines of Bible reading and prayer during the retreat.

Don't make notes during your prayer time, allowing God to have your full attention and trust that God will recall the important movements when you come to review your prayer time.

8. **Review of Prayer**   [Page 59f]

- ❏ This is likely to be a new experience for the retreatant.

- ❏ Need to stress the importance of this discipline during the retreat.

- ❏ Emphasise the break from the time of prayer, but not leaving too big a gap between the prayer time and the review. There should be only a "breathing space" between the time of prayer and the review – time to make a cuppa!

- ❏ Let the review recall to mind what God wants you to recall. It is God centred.

- ❏ Our feelings and desires are important to note in the review.

- ❏ The review is an opportunity to listen again to the time of prayer as you have journeyed with the Lord, noticing changes of mood, feelings, ideas and thoughts.

The following papers are explored and explained by the directors with their retreatants as and when applicable.

9. **Repetition in Prayer** [Page 62f]

This too is likely to be a new experience and discipline for the retreatant.

It is a means of returning to an experience of prayer and deepening the experience so helping us to listen more attentively to the Lord.

10. **Reviewing the Day** [Page 66f]

This is an important part of the retreat exercise and needs to be explained carefully. During the retreat, directors need to ensure that the retreatants are doing their Review of the Day.

11. A break for coffee and tea.

12. **An Exercise of Praying with Scripture**

- ❑ Begin by inviting the retreatants to:
    - sit comfortably.
    - close eyes - sitting comfortably and up straight.
    - listen to the sounds outside.
    - listen to the sounds inside the room.
    - become aware of your own breathing.
- ❑ Set the mood with some music.
- ❑ Read a passage of Scripture slowly several times.

- ❑ Listen to God speaking from the Word:

> *"The word of God is alive and active.*
> *It cuts more keenly than any two-edged*
> *sword, piercing so deeply that it divides*
> *soul and spirit, joints and marrow; it*
> *discriminates among the purposes and*
> *thoughts of the heart. Nothing in all*
> *creation can hide from him; everything*
> *lies bare and exposed to the eyes of*
> *him to whom we must render account"*
>
> *(Hebrews 4; 12 - 13)*

Suggested Passages of Scripture

Psalm 131	-	*A prayer of humble trust*
Jeremiah 29; 11 - 14	-	*God's plan for me*
Luke 19; 1 - 10	-	*Zacchaeus*
John 1; 35 - 42	-	*The first disciples*

- ❑ Read the passage of Scripture slowly.

- ❑ After a few minutes read the passage of Scripture again.

- ❑ Then again after some more silence: and even again.

As the exercise comes to an end:

- ❑ Invite people to share briefly, anything that strikes them from the passage:
  - -   a line.
  - -   a phrase.
  - -   a thought.

- ❑ If need be, begin yourself, or prepare the team to make a start.

- ❑ It may be useful to give a few brief ideas from the passage.

- ❑ After the retreatants have shared, invite anyone who wishes to offer a brief prayer - if need be begin yourself.

- ❑ Bring the exercise to a close with some more music.

13. Any questions from the whole group?

14. Give out lists of retreatants and the direction groups. The rest of the session is spent in direction groups.

Wish all well for the rest of the retreat.

15. **Direction Groups**

The Direction Groups move to their rooms:

- ❑ Start with simply getting to know each other.

- ❑ Seek to establish friendships in an un-threatening atmosphere.

- ❑ Invite any questions that may be in the retreatant's minds.

- ❑ Arrange times for interviews for the rest of the retreat.

- ❑ Give people their passages of Scripture to pray with for the next few days.

- ❑ Remind the retreatant that this retreat is a personal journey of faith and prayer and it is not helpful to "compare notes" with others along the way.

- ❑ End the evening when ready with some prayer together.

The Closing Session

The purpose of the final session of the retreat is to draw together the experience of the whole Month of Individually Guided Prayer in Everyday Life.

The hope will be:

- ❏ To appropriate the spiritual journey of the whole month.

- ❏ To give some guidance for the future, by way of Ongoing Prayer in Daily Life and the introduction of the practice of Praying at the End of the Day.

    - The Examen.

- ❏ To suggest some useful resources for prayer, including some suggested Scripture passages for the coming weeks.

- ❏ To explore the possibility of ongoing spiritual direction.

- ❏ To encourage a developing spirituality.

- ❏ To celebrate the gift of prayer and the community of which we have been part in the Lord.

Planning the Closing Session

Timing Two Hours Max

1.   Welcome -   together again after a month's journey of prayer.

2.   Explaining format of the session.

   ❑   An opportunity to be together again after our month of individual journey with the Lord.

   ❑   A time for sharing our experiences and exploring our encounters with the Lord during the month.

   ❑   Celebrate together with thanksgiving and with a simple Eucharist or Agape meal.

3.   The whole retreat group meets and in a relaxed and non-threatening atmosphere the group members are invited to share their own experiences of the retreat.

   -   invite the retreatant to share only what they want to share.

   -   enjoy some silence together.

   -   what has been the main experience during this month?

   -   how did the retreatants find the month?

   -   sharing will help us to 'own' the privilege of the prayer journey that has been our experience.

   -   to seek to explore the hope that is in the retreatants.

   -    help in continuing the journey of faith.

- encourage a full exchange.

- beware of the danger of divulging confidences.

- let the retreatants talk to each other.

- respect anyone's desire to be silent.

4. Where to from here?

❑ Whet appetite for input to come on continuing the prayer journey and experience of the past month.

❑ Be prepared for possible questions about future contact and desire for further spiritual direction.

5. Further additions to the retreatant's Folders can include the following if not already given to the retreatants by their directors towards the end of the retreat.

❑ **The Examen** (Page 77f)
offer and explain the use of the Examen. This may well have been already introduced during the Month of Individually Guided Prayer. But even so it is good once again to encourage this discipline of prayer.

❑ **Scriptures to Pray with in Everyday Life**
(Page 80)
a chance to offer some texts for the next three months at a rate of three texts for each week. We have found that three passages of Scripture a week have been helpful and using the Lectionary gives the retreatant appropriate Scripture for the Christian year.

❑ **Ongoing Prayer - Some suggestions** (Page 81)
a brief selection of Scripture passages for ongoing prayer on the theme – **Trust in God.**

❑ Distribute an evaluation sheet if they are to be used, stressing that they are not compulsory, but that they may help the retreatants' own appraisal of their journey and the retreat team as they plan further Months of Guided Prayer.

6.   Tea/Coffee

Take a break at this point for some refreshments and to allow the opportunity for the retreatants to talk to each other informally. Experience has shown that at the end of some Months or Weeks of Guided Prayer it has felt better to have refreshments after the Celebration at the end of the session.

7.   The Celebration

It is good to end the retreat with a brief Celebration. The Eucharist is the best known and accepted "Thanksgiving" of the Christian Church and is well placed at the end of a retreat. If it is difficult to arrange for a Communion to be shared then an Agape meal will equally provide a right ending to the retreat.

❑   Set the scene:

-    candles and music.

-    stillness exercise.

-    silence.

-    short Eucharist / Agape and/or brief time of sharing.

-    ending Music.

8. The Ending

Let the ending arise out of the Eucharist / Agape Celebration with an opportunity of valuing each other and the journey that has been shared over the past weeks.

- ❑ Avoid criticism at this point.

- ❑ Remind everyone that such a retreat is not the end but a beginning of an ongoing journey with God.

- ❑ Who can be told of this experience, who might like to share in it in the future? Share with the retreatants the fact that others are likely to find it extremely difficult to understand and appreciate the experience that they have just had in their month of guided prayer.

- ❑ Explore the possibility of ongoing Spiritual Direction.

- ❑ Final "thank yous".

- ❑ It may be right to offer the opportunity for a brief time of open or shared prayer.

9. Thank you to the hosts of the retreat.

10. Thank you on behalf of the direction team.

11. Final closing prayer.

SECTION THREE

Retreatant's Folder material

WELCOME

So,
you want to seek God with all your life,
and love Him with all your heart.

But you would be wrong
if you thought you could reach Him.
Your arms are too short, your eyes are too dim,
your heart and understanding too small.

To seek God
means first of all
to let yourself be found by Him.
He is the God of Abraham, Isaac and Jacob.
He is the God of Jesus Christ.
He is your God,
not because He is yours
but because you are His.

To choose God
is to realise that you are known and loved
in a way surpassing anything we can imagine,
loved before anyone had thought of you
or spoken your name.

To choose God
means giving yourself up to Him in faith.
Let your life be built on this faith
as on an invisible foundation.
Let yourself be carried by this faith
like a child in its mother's womb.

And so,
don't talk too much about God
but live
in the certainty that He has written your name
on the palm of his hand.

This piece has been adapted from "Rule for a New Brother"
Ed. Henri Nouwen, Published by DLT

A Month of Individually Guided Prayer

- We have come together in retreat for all sorts of reasons. In reality it is God who has brought us here.

  (John 6; 44)

- God's favourite word is "Come".
  He is personally inviting each one of us to come just as we are:
  - with our hopes, fears and worries.

  (Matthew 11; 28f)

- We come to spend time with Him:
  - in a special way.
  - in the midst of our ordinary lives.

- Come with an open mind and a generous spirit willing to let God surprise us.
  - He has His plans for us this month.

  (John 1; 35 - 39)

- We then need to let go of our plans and allow God's plans to unfold.

- Our time spent alone with God in prayer this month is the most important part of the retreat. The talks that we will have with our directors will help us to notice the movements in the journey, but the <u>real</u> Director will always be God.

❑ Let's begin by placing ourselves, our families, our work, our cares and concerns in the hands of the Lord, as we begin this retreat together.

❑ Let go.
   Let God.
      Pray for that grace.

❑ Let's pray for each other:
   others are praying for you.
   your directors are praying for you.

❑ Remember that your directors are ordinary people who will have their own ups and downs in prayer during this retreat.

❑ Let us pray for each other.

Praying with Scripture

The Prayer Time

This is the most important time:
- ❑ Everyone is different.
- ❑ We all need to pray as we can in our own way.
- ❑ You have been praying already in many different ways.
- ❑ It is God who teaches us how to pray.
- ❑ The Spirit prays in us, even when we feel we can't.

(Romans 8; 26 - 28)

- ❑ You cannot tell people how to make friends:
  - you can introduce them to each other.
  - the rest happens between the two of them.

- ❑ Prayer is being with God as a friend.

Waiting, Listening and Responding.

(Psalm 46; 10)

The function of prayer is not to establish a routine, but to explore our relationship with God who is always in relationship with us.

Entering Prayer

- Read the passage of Scripture before you come to your prayer time.
- Find a suitable Time and Place:
  - find the right place for you.
  - the place that fits your needs.
- Find a comfortable position - sitting, or kneeling.
- Try to have a straight back, but don't force it:
  - the best posture for you is what helps you to be attentive and relaxed at the same time.

Prayer is a Gift!
- All methods of prayer are means to an end:
  - no one method works for everyone.
  - find the one (or more than one) that helps you.
- Remember that all methods need practice before you become at home with them.
  - that means we need some patience with ourselves.

Opening ourselves to God

"I need to be still and let God love me
I need to relax and let God take over"

(African American Hymn)

Some Exercises to become still

Begin to relax:
- Close your eyes.
- Listen to the sounds all around you:
  - each sound is God's gift in this moment of your life.
  - celebrate the present moment.

- stay with the sounds nearest to you, even those in your own body.
- then gradually extend the field of your listening to the sounds in your room, in the house, garden and eventually listen to those sounds far away. All these are yours just now, and can be used to centre down into prayer.

❑ Now you may like to notice your own breathing:
- each breath is God's gift to you, the gift of His Spirit and life for you.
- be grateful for each breath that you take.
- become quiet in the Lord's presence.

❑ As you become relaxed:
- let that deep peace flow from the top of your head into your forehead.
- receive God's gift of life to you as you take your next breath.
- as you breathe out, breathe away any tensions in your forehead.

- let that feeling of peace flow into your face, into the small muscles around your eyes, nose, mouth.
- let your jaw relax.
- receive God's gift of life to you as you take your next breath.
- as you breathe out, breathe away any tensions in your face.

- let that feeling of peace flow into your neck, across your shoulders, down your upper arms, lower arms to your finger tips.
- receive God's gift of life to you as you take your next breath.

- as you breathe out, breathe away any tensions.
- with each breath you take, let the tensions of the day ebb away.
- with each breath you take, allow yourself to become as deeply relaxed and at peace.

- continue the journey down through your body relaxing your muscles.
- notice the tensions and where they are for you.
- down into your chest, tummy, trunk.
- down the front of your legs, into your ankles, into your feet, into your toes.

- receive God's gift of life to you as you take your next breath.
- as you breathe out, breathe away any tensions.

- then return to the top of your head.
- now journey down the back of your head into our neck, down your back, your buttocks, the back of your legs and into your feet and toes.

- receive God's gift of life to you as you take your next breath.
- as you breathe out, breathe away any tensions.

letting go and letting God be God

Let each intake of breath express your gratitude to the Lord and all that you long for from the Lord and let each out-breath be a surrender of your self to the Lord, together with all your worries, anxieties, guilt and pain.

If these exercises make you feel so relaxed that you become drowsy, then congratulations, you are doing really well!!

Concentrate not on your own endeavours but on God's love for you streaming into your life. Take a few moments to become aware of who you are going to be with.

Listen to God, who loves you just as you are, who calls you by name.

Surfacing your desires

Notice how you are feeling and what you desire most just now:

❑ Meet Jesus, the Risen Lord at the door way of your time of prayer and hear Him asking you: "What do you want?"

❑ What do you really want in this time of prayer?

❑ Surface your desire!

❑ It may be quite obvious to you what you want:
  - peace.
  - healing.
  - an answer to a pressing question.

❑ Or you may be at a loss to answer the question:
  - it may be just that you don't know what you want and you simply just want to be here with the Lord in your time of prayer.

❑ Whatever it is:
  - answer the question "What do you want?
    (Matthew 7; 7 - 11)

❑ So we begin by asking God to teach you how to pray:
  - be open to Him in your thoughts and in the generosity of your heart.

- ❏ Take your time getting ready.

- ❏ Relax.

The Centre of Prayer

Read the passage slowly.
Notice and listen attentively to every word.

- ❏ What ever passage you have chosen, or been given:
  - take your time to relax.
  - come to it as you are.
  - notice your mood, your feelings.
  - this is the real you that God wants to be with in your prayers.

- ❏ Don't try to work things out:
  - it's not a Bible study.

- ❏ Let God speak to you:
  - let it be His agenda, not yours!

- ❏ Take time to read the passage really slowly. Let its moods meet you where you are, don't try to work at it, or find deep and hidden meanings in it. Just be with it, open and generous to what God might want to be saying to you and in you. You will probably need to read the passage several times, then put it on one side and just wait upon God to pray in you in the way that God knows will open you up to Him.

- ❏ How do you feel and how do you respond?

Sometimes, as you read the passage again and again, it may be that a word or a phrase captures your attention:
- ❏ You are drawn to it, you notice it, it calls to you.
- ❏ Don't rush on, but stay with it.
- ❏ Let it speak to you, relish it, hold it, ask questions of it, let it be deep within you.

❑ You may be led to other images or thoughts, pictures or ideas, memories or experiences from your own life's journey, all stemming from this one word, or phrase.

❑ You may just simply want to stay with it in stillness and in its mystery.

One way to read Scripture in prayer is to read it as you would read a letter from a very dear friend, you read it again and again, re-reading parts of it, again and again. Savouring and enjoying what is special to you now.

❑ Stop wherever you feel drawn to stop!

❑ You don't have to complete anything!

❑ Respond as you feel you want to respond!

(Hebrews 4; 12 - 13)

Sometimes, as you read the passage again and again, you may find yourself entering into a scene or part of the story as if you were really there. Such experience of prayer using the gift of your imagination has a long and honoured history in the Christian tradition. Trust the Spirit of God working in you to lead you in your imagination.

❑ See, the place, the people, the events.

❑ Touch, smell, feel, look and listen to what is going on in the scene.

❑ Notice what is going on in you, your feelings and your desires.

❑ Who are you with in the scene, what is this all saying to you in your own life experience?

❑ Don't worry about the distractions, they happen to us all.

❑ Don't worry about your wanderings, or if you go to sleep.

❑ All this is part of prayer.

❑ Simply come back to the Scripture passage and read it again and again, enjoying the living Word of God.

❑ Let the Lord speak to you in the now of your life.

(Isaiah 55; 3)

❑ Don't write anything down.
Just be with the Lord and let the prayer take its own course.

❑ As your time of prayer comes to an end, just take a few minutes to be with Jesus, or with God The Father, or with the Holy Spirit, be with them just as one good friend is with another.

❑ Chat through your feelings:
- recall the striking thoughts that came your way.
- what were those pictures, ideas?

❑ How were you when the prayer began?
- what were you looking for?
- how do you feel now?

❑ In all of this the Lord has been at work, deep in you.

Loving you, because God is Love.

Close of Prayer

❑ Give the full time to your prayer.

❑ Don't be tempted to give up before the end of the half - hour.

❑ Don't keep going for longer, just because it feels good.

❑ Then take your leave graciously, just as you might when leaving a very dear friend with thanksgiving and goodbyes.
- you might like to use a familiar prayer,
  or a verse of Scripture like the
  "Our Father ..."

Review of Prayer

After the time of prayer, review that prayer time with the Lord.

- ❑ First take a break <u>briefly:</u>
  - change your position.
  - make a cup of tea/coffee.
  - have a short walk.

- ❑ Then sit down with your Prayer Journal:
  - note the date, the passage that you chose and your desire.

- ❑ Ask the Lord to re-collect for you the important movements, feelings and ideas of your prayer time.

- ❑ Allow a quarter of the time spent in prayer for your review, you don't have to be writing all the time.

- ❑ Let the Lord re-mind you of your time with Him.

So jot down in your Prayer Journal what happened to you, what you did and what you experienced.

- ❑ Don't make any judgements.

- ❑ Don't try to analyse your experience.

- ❑ Just note it down, as the Lord re-calls it for you.

For example:-

- how did I start the time of prayer?
- what was I feeling?
- what were my desires?
- what went on?
- what struck me - ideas etc.?
- were there any strong feelings or emotions?
        e.g. joy, anxiety, fear, boredom etc.
- was I distracted a great deal?
- if so, in what way did it happen?
- did my mood change?
- did I go to sleep?
- what did the Lord show me and how did I react?
- is there something I want to return to?

Thank the Lord for His goodness and if need be, be sorry for any negligence.

You may find only one or two things to note down, or you may be overwhelmed with material.

Whether it is a little or a lot, give the full time to your Review.

The Review helps you to notice the movement of your interior encounter with the Lord, not just intellectually in the mind, but in the feelings and the heart.

Do not make notes during your prayer time because that might well interrupt the flow of the prayer.

Let happen what is happening with the Lord.

Afterwards take a look in the Review, to see what the Lord was doing with you!

Two Examples

The Review of Prayer can be seen to be like:

> Imagining that you are sitting alone after a long visit with a great friend.
>
> The two of you have covered a lot of ground.
>
> You might have talked a bit about politics, about other friends, about your own long-established friendship.
>
> As you sit remembering, you recall certain sentences that one or other of you said, and identify feelings you had at certain junctures.
>
> You know "what you talked about" and can name the general feeling of your time together, good or wonderful, painful or exciting.
>
> You know that there are still things unresolved and unfinished, things still to be said.
>
> When you make a Review of Prayer, you do very much the same thing.

Or you could try taking the "climate" of your prayer:

> A still summer afternoon?   A stormy winter's night?
>
> A breezy morning?   A very, very dull long afternoon?
>
> A cold winter's night?   A beautiful clear morning?
>
> A miserable wet and foggy day?

Repetition

Deepening your prayer experience

Don't be in a hurry to move on to other passages or new prayer exercises.

- ❑ Repetition allows you to listen more attentively to the Lord, to hear again, to listen again to what the Lord was saying.

Repetition is not

- ❑ going back over the same material for prayer, as one repeats a school exercise to understand it better.
- ❑ nor is it a returning to the same piece of Scripture, in order to dig up something new or different.
- ❑ neither is it a returning to the <u>whole</u> Scripture passage of your last prayer period.

Repetition is

- ❑ a returning to those moments where you were particularly moved, that you noted in the Review of Prayer:
  - either positively or negatively.

Note the importance of the Review here!

So it is not a returning to the whole of Scripture given, or to the whole experience itself.

It is returning to the points where the experience occurred.

So for your next period of prayer return to the key areas of feelings and insights which you noted down in your Review.

- ❏ Begin by staying with, enjoying and relishing what was most energising or life giving for you in your previous time of prayer.

- ❏ Stay with those feelings, those ideas and let them find a deep and lasting place in you.

- ❏ Let them settle in you, affirming you and building you up.

- ❏ Drink deeply from that well of love that you experienced in your prayer time and be refreshed and thankful.

You may then want to return to your Review and read it slowly once again and notice anything which was less comfortable, more of a challenge.

- ❏ Ask the Lord if by staying here He desires to reveal something which needs to be owned, befriended or forgiven.

- ❏ If you feel the need to read on, then do so, always open to the leading of the Spirit which may bring you back to the same point you have just left.

- ❏ You may need to just be prepared to stay there and wait for the Lord's leading and love in that situation.

What does Repetition Do?

- ❏ It helps us to listen more carefully to God.

- ❏ It allows us to go back to where we were conscious of God's engagement with us and there listen again to His words and His leading.

- ❏ It allows us to become aware of those interior spiritual movements that are taking place in the retreat and in our life of prayer.

By allowing us time, it allows God time

- ❏ Many of our interior reactions in prayer happen unnoticed.

- ❏ Repetition gives time for those reactions to be experienced more distinctly.

- ❏ It helps us to respect God's communicating.

- ❏ It helps us grow from desolation to consolation.

Just because our prayer time has come to an end, it does not mean that God has finished His work with us.

Hurrying on to another passage can distract us from listening to what God is saying to us in our prayers.

When facing struggle, distractions and boredom in prayer it will be only too easy to reject the experience as empty or worthless.
But Repetition may reveal that those very negative experiences are in fact God speaking at a deeper level and we are resisting Him.

If we can return to the point where we first experienced those feelings of "negativity", we often find that the Lord has overcome that barrier, and desolation gives way to consolation; darkness to light; struggle to surrender.

It helps us become
            quieter
                    simpler
                            deeper

        more truly contemplative
                open to God and His desires
                        and then more able to make a loving
                                response to Him.

This exercise may seem very strange at first for it is not so much an exercise for our heads to look for the right or wrong answers in our experience, but an opportunity to explore more fully the reaction of our instincts and feelings.

It is simple, yet profound and, like any simple task, learning it can seem complicated.

        Persevere and we will find that God is truly a God of
                surprises.

Reviewing the Day

At the end of the day we often find ourselves mulling over events and experiences of the day.

In a retreat it is good to take this time and use it as a simple prayer exercise. This short time of reflection can be done at any time, and builds on that natural tendency of mulling over the day.

What is ever so important here is, instead of making our own judgements and analysis of the day, we ask the Lord to show us

> "to bring to our consciousness"

how the Creative Spirit of God has been working in our experiences and in our lives.

How can we do this?

- ❑ Take some time to relax - feel attentive and open and be thankful.

- ❑ Ask the Lord to show you where He has been active in your life today.

- ❑ Let the day play itself back to you:
  - in any order.
  - allow the moments and events which you enjoyed come to mind.
  - don't scratch around for information.
  - just wait and let it come to you in its own good time and in what ever order and how ever insignificant it may seem.

- ❑ Let the feelings of these moments, events, people, be really felt.

❑ Revisit the experience, taking time to relish it.

❑ Take as long as you want.

❑ Let the day play itself back to you once again:
- this time ask the Lord for enlightenment about the various moods and feelings of your day, especially where those moods changed for good or bad.

❑ Let yourself feel what you felt:
- it may help to express it.
- feel what you felt.

❑ Where did that mood or feeling come from?
- where did that mood or feeling take me?
- did it feel a creative movement?
- was it life giving?
- was I being driven or drawn?
- did it lead to life denying actions or behaviour?
- what underlying attitudes are being revealed to me?

❑ What do I want to own and express which needs befriending and healing?

❑ What choices does this reflection time reveal to me about tomorrow?

❑ What about tomorrow's journey?
- where will I be taken with the Lord tomorrow?
- what will be driving me?
- what will be drawing me?

N.B. *Resist the voice of your inner critic and let God show you all the nudges to greater life in the glorious imperfect human being that you are!*

Some texts that may be helpful for settling into the Retreat

"As a deer longs for a stream of cool water so
 my soul longs after you, O my God.
 Psalm 42; 1–2

"O God, you are my God, and I long for you."
 Psalm 63; 1 – 5

"O God you search me and you know me."
 Psalm 139

"The Sovereign Lord, the holy one of Israel
 (your name), says: "Come back and quietly
 trust in me."...
 The Lord is waiting to be merciful to you."
 Isaiah 30; 15, 18

"The Lord, the King of Israel (your name), is
 with you; there is no reason now to be
 afraid."
 Zephaniah 3; 15b – 18a

"Come to me, all you who are weary and
 burdened, and I will give you rest."
 Matthew 11; 28

"When Jesus saw John's disciples following
 him, he asked, "What are you looking for?"
 "Rabbi, where are you staying?" they asked.
 "Come !" replied Jesus, "and you will see."
 John 1; 35 - 42

"I wait patiently for God to save me; . . .
Trust in him at all times, my people. (your name);
Psalm 62; 1 – 2, 5 – 8

"Come, everyone who is thirsty – here is water!"
Isaiah 55; 1 – 11

"I alone know the plans I have for you, declares the Lord."
Jeremiah 29; 11 – 14

"Do not be afraid, little flock (your name), for your Father is pleased to give you the Kingdom."
Luke 12; 32

SECTION FOUR

Retreatant's Folder material

for the end of the retreat

As the Retreat ends . . . .

Spend some time reflecting on some of the following

- ❑ What has God shown me about himself during these days?
- ❑ What has God shown me about myself during the retreat?
- ❑ What has God been inviting me to?
- ❑ How have I responded to the movement of God in me?
- ❑ What fears and resistances have I experienced?
- ❑ What hopes and desires have I felt within me?
- ❑ What implications does this retreat have for my daily life?
- ❑ What do I want to ask God at this time?

Spend a little time thanking God for all that has happened.

The following scripture passages may help at this time:

I know the plans I have in mind for you, it is God who speaks. Plans for peace not disaster, reserving a future full of hope for you. Then when you call to me and come to be with me I will listen to you. When you seek me with all you heart I shall let you find me.
Jeremiah 29; 11 – 13

Do not be afraid, for I am with you;
I have called you by name and you are mine.
Isaiah 43; 1

Does a woman forget her baby at her breast, or fail to cherish the child in her womb? Yet even if these forget, I will never forget you.
See, I have carved your name on the palm of my hand.
Isaiah 49; 15 – 16

Take up your cross and follow me!
Mark 8; 34

. . . she knew what had happened to her.
Mark 5; 33

Even if your heart condemns you,
God is greater than your heart and he knows everything.
1 John 3; 20

Ongoing Prayer in Everyday Life

We have all had a very special experience over this past month.

Now where do we go?

How can we continue to pray in our ordinary lives?

There are many ways of praying:

- ❑ Prayer is about our relationship with God.
- ❑ No two people are the same, nor do they have the same relationship with God.
- ❑ Each person has his/her own unique way of praying.
- ❑ And at times one way of praying will suit better than another.
- ❑ At any time we may use any number of different ways of praying.

Be Realistic

We have been trying to pray for thirty minutes or more each day. We may well want to continue that in some way.

That's often impossible so:

- Be realistic.

Try to decide how many minutes you can actually give to prayer each day - even if it is only five or ten minutes each day.

If some days it just does not happen:

- Don't give up!

Time and Place

Having decided to pray each day or a few times each week:

- ❏ Find a suitable Time and Place.

- ❏ Maybe a little corner in your home:
  - a simple place.
  - a holy place.
  - go to that place to pray.

Be Still

Make yourself comfortable and become still:

- ❏ Give yourself plenty of time.

- ❏ Listen to your world:

  - sounds inside and outside.

- ❏ Listen to yourself:

  - your own breathing.

  - your desires and feelings.

- ❏ Offer a short prayer:

  - "Lord, teach me to pray".

Review

Keep your Prayer Journal going:

- ❏ Review your time with the Lord.

- ❏ Give a quarter of the time spent in prayer to your review.

❑   Ask the Lord to re-collect your prayer experience.

From time to time use your Prayer Journal as material for
reflection.

Remember

Prayer is a relationship with God, like all relationships it
has its ups and downs, we learn to pray by praying. Pray as
you can - not as you can't.

❑   God is found in the now:
   -        in distractions.
   -        in wanderings and concerns.

❑   Sometimes when we are very low all we can do is just
    give the time and trust that the Spirit will pray in us.
                                            (Romans 8; 26f)

Prayer is a gift. We can't make it happen on our own.

❑   Ask often for this gift:
   -        "Lord, teach me to pray".

❑   Know that God always wants to give us this gift.

The Examen

"Lord, you have examined me and you know me.
You know me at rest and in action;
You discern my thoughts from afar.
You trace my journeying and my resting-places,
and are familiar with all the paths I take."

[Psalm 139; 1 - 3]

❑ Relax and thank the Lord for today:

- for all that has gone to make up my day.

- it has all been a gift from the Lord.

- I myself am God's greatest gift to me.

- I am the gift by which I can know every other gift.

Spend a few moments becoming aware of my need to just be grateful.

❑ Ask the Holy Spirit to help me to see what He wants me to see of today's journey:

- so it's not my analysis of the day which is important.

- nor is it my judgement on the day.

- rather it is the Spirit who reveals God's truth and love to me.

❑ Recall in the quiet, the day that has been mine:

- let the day play itself back, in whatever order as I let things surface in my prayer.

- remember the places I've been in.

- the activities I've been part of.

- see the people I was with today.

❑ Ask the Lord to show me where He was present in me and in others:

- he has been acting with me where His Spirit has been at work.

- I notice the footprints of God in my day.

- where have I been aware of::

> *love, joy, peace, patience,*
> *kindness, goodness, faithfulness,*
> *gentleness, and self-control.*
> *[Galatians 5; 22]*

- where I was able to be open to the work of the Spirit: I give thanks.

- where I closed myself to God's presence: I ask for forgiveness.

❑ Deepening my prayer

- ask the Lord for strength to know His will in my day and the grace to respond to Him.

- to be more aware of where I failed to notice Him in my day.

- to know where He did not manage to work with me and in me, or through me with and for others.

- to be glad where I was in harmony with Him and co-operated with His gifts in me.

❑ Looking ahead to a new day and take a look at tomorrow:

- ask for grace to see the way of the Lord in my new day.

- the places I will be in.

- the people I will be with.

- the activities I will be involved in:
  e.g. with this person I will need the gift of patience;
        in this place I will need perseverance;
        with these people I will need gentleness.

❑ Ask the Lord for what I see I will need:

- ask very simply, very humbly and trusting in the loving presence of the Father, Son, and Holy Spirit.

NOTE

This prayer, with practice and in time will do wonders for you, as you grow in sensitivity, to notice God's presence with you, moment by moment, becoming more and more able

to find God in all things.

Scriptures to Pray With

Here are three suggested Scriptures for each week.

Use any, or all of them as you want to, when you want to.

Make one or two Repetitions of them in your praying as you want. Be realistic in your praying time.
If you miss or give up for a time:
   - don't worry   - come back to it when you can.

Week beginning:

October 10th.
   Psalm 23
   Philippians 4; 4 - 9
   Matthew 22; 1 - 14

October 17th.
   Psalm 96
   Exodus 33; 12 - 23
   Luke 10; 25 - 37

October 24th.
   Jeremiah 29; 11 - 14
   Ephesians 6; 10 - 20
   John 4; 46 - 54

October 31st.
   Psalm 130
   Ephesians 2; 13 - 22
   Matthew 18; 21 – 35

November 7th.
   Psalm 105; 1 - 11
   Isaiah 11; 1 - 10
   Matthew 5; 1 - 10

November 14th.
   Ezekiel 37; 1 - 14
   Romans 8; 31 - 39
   Mark 5; 21 - 43

November 21st.
   Psalm 116; 12 - 19
   Colossians 1; 13 - 20
   John 6; 1 - 14

November 28th.
   Hosea 11; 1 -11
   2 Corinthians 5; 14 - 6;2
   Matthew 25; 31 - 46

December 5th.
   Psalm 95
   Isaiah 40; 1 - 11
   Luke 4; 14 - 21

December 12th.
   Isaiah 35; 1 - 10
   1 Thessalonians 5; 16 - 24
   Luke 1; 26 - 38

December 19th.
   Isaiah 52; 1 - 10
   Luke 1; 46 - 55
   Luke 2; 1 - 7

December 26th.
   Isaiah 9; 2 - 7
   Luke 2; 8 -20
   Matthew 2; 1 - 12

January 2nd.
   Isaiah 61; 1 - 4
   John 1; 1 - 5, 10 - 14
   John 1; 16 - 18

January 9th.
   Jeremiah 1; 4 - 10
   Mark 1; 14 - 20
   Philippians 1; 3 - 11

EXAMPLE

"The Lord be with you."

Ongoing Prayer

Some Suggestions

Some suggestions for further texts for contemplative
Prayer on the theme of Trust in God.

Psalm 23	*The Lord is my shepherd*
Psalm 27	*With God there is no fear*
Psalm 121	*Guarding*
Psalm 131	*A simple trust*
Psalm 139	*God's complete knowledge*
Isaiah 43 1 - 5	*Do not be afraid . . .*
Isaiah 49; 13 - 1	*Never forgetting*
Hosea 11; 1 - 4, 8 - 9	*I led them (and you) . . .*
Matthew 11; 28 - 30	*"Come to me . . ."*
Luke 1; 26 - 38	*The Annunciation*
Luke 12; 22 - 32	*Providence*
John 14; 1 - 10	*"Remain in my love . . . "*
John 15	*Abiding*
John 20; 19 - 31	*The Risen Lord*
John 21; 15 - 20	*"Do you love me . . ."*
Romans 8; 14 - 18, 26 - 39	*The gift of the Spirit*
1 Corinthians 1; 18 - 30	*Power*
2 Corinthians 4; 16 - 5; 2	*Renewal*
Galatians 2; 6 - 7	*Union*
1 Peter 2; 1 - 10	*Living stones*
Revelation21; 1 - 7	*All things new*

There are many more.

SECTION FIVE

Extra non-biblical material for accompanying others

Extra Material

As we share another person's journey of prayer in a Retreat in Everyday Life it may be useful from time to time to use other material together with Scripture. We have had the very real privilege of walking alongside some people who find themselves in situations where the Bible has become a difficult book, others have deeply valued non-biblical material as sources for their meditations. Yet others have been unable to read, or have limited reading skills, for these retreatants pictures and icons have proved powerful tools for prayer. For others music can be a deeply rewarding resource for their times of prayer.

I have not been able to include in this publication a selection of pictures or icons, but invite you to explore the great treasury of religious and contemporary art and music as yet more material for the accompaniment of others in their prayer journeys.

For some retreatants the use of their own skills of painting, writing, modelling and even gardening have all proved to be valuable aids to prayer. For others the invitation and even permission to pray has opened long closed doors of inner joy and spiritual growth.

The following is a small selection of meditations and poetry that have proved to be useful aids in the practice of walking alongside a retreatant in their time of prayer.

Many of these pieces have come my way without designation. Some have been given to me on my own prayer retreats. Others have been offered to me by fellow directors and for that I am extremely grateful. I have endeavoured to ascertain the necessary copyright details for as many as possible. I am very much aware that I may well have missed a number and for this I make my confession and present my apologies and would be delighted to know where I have failed so that I can make amends in any further publication of this document.

Settle yourself in solitude

and you will come upon God

in yourself

Teresa of Avila (1515 -82)

****

Be
do not do
or pretend to be
anything.
Just be.

Be still.
Calm those
anxious, unruly
whirling thoughts
into stillness.

Be still and know
as the flower knows the sun's rays,
as the mouth knows bread,
as the heart knows love,
open yourself
to knowing.

Be still and know that I am
here and now
around you and within you,
behind you and before you
wherever you are,
I am.

Be still and know that I am God
your Father and Mother
your Companion and Healer
your Life and your All.

Be
Be still
Be still and know
Be still and know that I am
God.

Muddy water,

Let stand,

Becomes clear.

Lao Tse (5th. Cent. B.C.)

****

Let your God love you

Be silent
Be still.
Alone, Empty
Before your God
Say nothing.
Ask nothing.
Be silent.
Be still

Let your God
Look upon you.
That is all.
He knows.
He understands.
He loves you with
An enormous love.
He only wants to
Look upon you
With His Love.
Quiet.
Still.
Be.

Let your God -
Love you.

Spirit of Freedom

Inside each of us
there awaits
a wonder
full
spirit of freedom

                        she awaits
                        to dance
                        in the rooms
                        of our heart
                        that are closed
                        dark and cluttered

she waits
to dance
in the spaces
where negative feelings
have built barricades
and stock-piled weapons

                        she waits
                        to dance
                        in the corners
                        where we still
                        do not believe
                        in our goodness

inside each of us
there awaits
a wonder
full
spirit of freedom

                        she will lift light feet
                        and make glad songs
                        within us
                        on the day
                        we open the door of ego
                        and let the enemies
                        stomp out

Joyce Rupp

Now

I was regretting the past
       and fearing the future

Suddenly my Lord was speaking

"MY NAME IS - I AM"

He paused

I waited

He continued

"When you live in the past
with its mistakes and regrets
it is hard.
I am not there.

My name is not I WAS.

When you live in the future
With its problems and fears
It is hard.
I am not there.

My name is not I WILL BE.

When you live in <u>this</u> moment
It is not hard.
I am here

My name is I AM."

THANK YOU LORD

HELP ME TO GROW IN TRUST

Slow me down Lord

Slow me down Lord,

Ease the pounding of my heart by the quietening of my mind,

Steady my hurried pace with the vision of the eternal reach of time.

    Give me, amid the confusion of the day,

        the calmness of the everlasting hills.

    Break the tension of my nerves and muscles

        with the soothing music of the singing streams

        that live in my memory ...

Slow me down Lord, and inspire me to send my roots

        deep into the soil of life's enduring values,

    that I may grow towards my greater destiny.

    Remind me each day that the race is not always to the swift;

    that there is more to life than increasing its speed.

Orin L. Crain

****

Give me a scallop-shell of quiet,

  My staff of faith to walk upon,

    My script of joy, immortal diet,

      My bottle of salvation,

        My gown of glory, hope's true gage,

          And thus I'll take my pilgrimage.

Sir Walter Ralegh (c. 1552 - 1618)

Prayer of Abandonment

Father, I abandon myself into your hands

Do with me what you will.

Whatever you do, I will thank you.

I am ready for all, I accept all.

Let your will be done in me and in all your creatures.

This only I ask, Lord.

Father, I offer myself to you with all the love of my heart.

For I love you, Lord,

      and therefore need to give myself to you,

      to surrender myself into your hands

         without reserve

         and with boundless confidence.

For you are my Father.

Charles de Foucauld (1858 - 1916)

****

God in our image

Invariably we create a God in our own image.

Because we do not love him very much,
we are led to think he does not love us much.

Because we do not worry much about him,
we imagine that he does not worry very much about us

Because we are not very happy with him,
we conclude that he is not very happy with us.

Gerard Hughes S.J.

God ... is found when He is sought and when

He is no longer sought He escapes.

He is heard only when we hope to hear Him,

and if thinking our hope to be fulfilled,

we cease to listen, He ceases to speak.

His silence ceases to be vivid and becomes dead,

even though we recharge it with the echo

of our own emotional noise.

Thomas Merton (1915 - 1968)

****

I know from experience that
'the Kingdom of heaven is within you'.
Jesus has no need of books or teachers to instruct the souls.
He teaches without the noise of words.
Never have I heard him speak,
but I feel that he is within me at each moment:
he is guiding and inspiring me with what I must say and do.
I find just when I need them certain lights which I had not
    seen until then,
and it isn't most frequent during my hours of prayer
that these are most abundant
but in the midst of my daily occupations.

Therese of Lisieux (1873 - 1897)

Give me a candle of the Spirit, O God,
as I go down into the deep of my own being.
Show me the hidden things.
Take me down to the spring of my life,
and tell me my nature and my name.

Give me freedom to grow
so that I may become my true self -
the fulfilment of the seed which you planted in
me at my awakening.

Out of the deep I cry unto thee, O God.
Amen.

George Appleton

****

Let me rise - and adore you

God, let me rise to the edges of time and
        open my life to your eternity;
let me run to the edges of space and
        gaze into your immensity;
let me climb through the barriers of sound and
        pass into your silence;
And then, in stillness and silence
        let me adore You,
Who are Life - Light - Love -
        without beginning and without end,
the Source - the Sustainer - the Restorer -
        the Purifier - of all that is;
the Love who has bound earth to heaven
        by the beams of a cross;
the Healer who has renewed a dying race
        by the blood of a chalice;
the God who has taken humanity into your glory
        by the wounds of sacrifice;
God ... God ... God ... Blessed be God
        Let me adore you.   Amen.

Sister Ruth SLG, OBP

Earth's crammed with heaven,
     and every common bush afire with God;
But only he who sees take off his shoes,
     the rest sit round it and pick blackberries,
And daub their natural faces unaware
     more and more from the first similitude

Elizabeth Barrett Browning

****

Be still!
Shut out life's jangling, noisy sounds awhile,
Within your inner sanctuary bid them cease;
Take time to bow beneath my welcoming smile
And learn to be at peace.

Be still!
Your busyness and ceaseless industry,
The rush and bustle of your daily round
Will sap your strength. So learn to rest in me
In whom all peace is found.

Be still!
The fear that makes you want to run away,
The inner struggle deep within your soul,
The danger threatening your future way -
Is under my control.

Be still!
Through quiet worship inner strength will grow;
By patient waiting paths will be made clear;
And those who humbly look to me will know
The love that casts out fear.

Be still!
For in the quiet place I gently heal,
Refreshing and renewing mind and soul;
And those who in my presence daily kneel
Return to life made whole.

Peter Tongeman

A Hymn to God the Father

Wilt thou forgive that sin where I begun,
  Which is my sin, though it were done before?
Wilt thou forgive those sins through which I run,
  And do then still, though still I do deplore?
      When thou hast done, thou hast not done,
        For I have more.

Wilt thou forgive that sin by which I won
  Others to sin, and made my sin their door?
Wilt thou forgive that sin which I did shun
  A year or two, but wallowed in a score?
      When thou has done, thou hast not done,
        For I have more.

I have a sin of fear, that when I've spun
  My last thread, I shall perish on the shore;
Swear by thyself that at my death thy Sun
  Shall shine as it shines now, and heretofore;
      And having done that, thou hast done,
        I have no more.

John Donne (1572 - 1631)

****

My Dear God,

I have no idea where I am going.
I do not see the road ahead of me.
I cannot know for certain where it will end.
Nor do I really know myself,
    and the fact that I think that I am following your will
    does not mean that I am actually doing so.
But I believe that the desire to please you does in fact please you.
And I hope I have that desire in all that I am doing.
I hope that I will never do anything apart from that desire.
And I know that if I do this you will lead me by the right road
    though I may not know anything about it.
Therefore I will trust you always
    though I may seem to be lost and in the shadow of death.
I will not fear, for you are ever with me,
        and you will never leave me to face my perils alone.

Thomas Merton

Love bade me welcome

Love bade me welcome: yet my soul drew back,
        Guilty of dust and sin.
But quick-eyed Love, observing me grow slack
        From my first entrance in,
Drew near to me, sweetly questioning
        If I lacked anything.

"A guest", I answered, "worthy to be here."
        Love said, "You shall be he."
"I the unkind, the ungrateful? Ah, my dear,
        I cannot look on Thee."
Love took my hand, and smiling did reply,
        "Who made the eyes but I?"

"Truth, Lord, but I have marred them: let my shame
        Go where it doth deserve."
"And know you not," says Love, "who bore the blame?"
        "My dear, then I will serve."
"You must sit down," says Love, "and taste my meat,"
        So did I sit and eat.

George Herbert (1593 -1633)

****

Our deepest fear is not that we are inadequate.
It is that we are powerful beyond measure.
It is our light, not our darkness, that most frightens us.

We ask ourselves
    "who am I to be brilliant, gorgeous, talented, fabulous?"
Actually,   Who are you not to be?

You are a child of God. Your playing small doesn't save the world.
There's nothing enlightened about shrinking so that other
        people won't feel insecure around you.

We are all meant to shine, as children do.
We were born to make manifest the glory of the universe
        that is within us.
And as we let our own light shine, we unconsciously give
        other people permission to do the same.
As we're liberated from our own fear, our presence
        automatically liberates others.

Nelson Mandela

I bid you but be:
I have need not of prayer.
I have need of you free
as your mouths of mine air,
that my heart may be greater within me,
   beholding
     the fruits of me, fair.

O my children, too dutiful
towards Gods not of me!
Was not I enough beautiful?
Was it hard to be free?
For behold: I am with you,
   am in you and of you.
     Look forth now and see.

"Hertha"
Charles Swinburne

****

Prayer

The way I most often express it is that there comes a level of prayer where it is no longer a question of "are you seeing something?" but "are you being seen?" - if you like, sitting in the light and of just being and becoming who you really are..

What a lot of the literature talks about is a sort of gathering-in of awareness into your self, which sounds a strange way of putting it, but it simply means our thoughts and fantasies are usually all over the place and running off after this, that and the other, and part of the process that is going on is the sort of steady and quiet drawing in and settling of all these tentacles that are wriggling out to lay hold of the world - you gather them back in and that's a gathering into the heart which the Orthodox writers talk about, and what Western writers mean by the simplification of heart in prayer. By this we simply become what we are and just sit there being a creature in the hand of God.

Dr. Rowan Williams

On Prayer

The Lord Jesus Himself will teach you how you should pray. His is the creative Word which you may receive in the silence of your heart and the fruitful soil of your life. Listen attentively to what He will say; be swift to carry out what He will ask of you. You have been promised His Spirit who will bear your poor little efforts before the throne of grace and into the intimacy of the living God.

Your prayer is therefore not so much a duty as a privilege; a gift rather than a problem or the result of your own efforts. So don't tire yourself out looking for beautiful thoughts or words, but stay attentive before God in humility and expectation, in desire and purity of heart, full of joy and hope. Your prayer will take countless forms because it is the echo of your life, and a reflection of the inexhaustible light in which God dwells.

Sometimes you will taste and see how good the Lord is. Be glad then, and give Him all honour, because His goodness to you has no measure. Sometimes you will be dry and joyless like parched land or an empty well. But your thirst and helplessness will be your best prayer if you accept them with patience and embrace them lovingly.

Sometimes your prayer will be an experience of the infinite distance that separates you from God; sometimes your being and His fullness will flow into each other. Sometimes you will be able to pray only with your body and hands and eyes; sometimes your prayer will move beyond words and images; sometimes you will be able to leave everything beyond you to concentrate on God and His Word. Sometimes you will be able to do nothing but take your whole life and everything in you and bring them before God. Every hour has its own possibilities of genuine prayer.

Taken from "Rule for a new Brother"
Ed. Henri Nouwen, Published by DLT

Disclosure

Prayer is like watching for the
    Kingfisher. All we can do is
Be where he is likely to appear and
        Wait.
Often, nothing happened;
    There is space, silence and
        Expectancy.
No visible sign, only the
Knowledge that he's been there,
    And may come again.
Seeing or not seeing ceases to matter,
    You have been prepared.
But sometimes, when you've almost
    Stopped expecting it
    A flash of brightness
    Gives encouragement.

Ann Lewin,   from "Candle and Kingfishers"

Flame, alive, compelling, yet tender past all telling,
    reaching the secret centre of my soul!
Since now evasion's over, finish your work, my Lover,
    break the last thread,
    wound me and make me whole!

Burn that is for my healing! Wound of delight past feeling!
    Ah, gentle hand whose touch is a caress,
Foretaste of heaven conveying and every debt repaying:
    slaying, you give me life for death's distress.

O lamps of fire bright-burning with splendid brilliance,
    turning deep caverns of my soul to pools of light!
Once shadowed, dim, unknowing,
    now their strange new-found glowing
    gives warmth and radiance for my Love's delight.

Ah! gentle and so loving you wake within me, proving
    that you are there in secret and alone;
Your fragrant breathing stills me,
    your grace, your glory fills me
    so tenderly your love becomes my own.

"Living Flame of Love",   St. John of the Cross (1542 - 1591)

The Lord God Says:

I myself will dream a dream within you
Good dreams come from me you know;
My dreams seem impossible, not too practical,
Not for the cautious man or woman;
A little risky sometimes, a trifle brash perhaps.

But some of my friends prefer to rest more
comfortably in sounder sleep with visionless eyes.

But for those who share my dreams I ask
A little patience,
A little humour,
Some small courage,
And a listening heart -
I will do the rest.

Then they will risk, and wonder at their daring,
Run, and marvel at their speed,
Build, and stand in awe at the beauty of their building;

You will meet me often as you work,
In your companions who share your risk
In your friends who believe in you enough
To lend their own dreams, their own hands,
Their own hearts, to your building,
In the people who will find your doorway,
Stay awhile,
And walk away knowing that they too can find a dream.

There will be sunfilled days,
And sometimes a little rain - a little variety
Both come from me.
So come now, be content
It is my dream, you dream,
My house you build
My caring you witness
My love you share
And this is the heart of the matter.

Charles Peguy

God's Grandeur

The world is charged with the grandeur of God.
　　It will flame out, like shining from shook foil;
　　It gathers to a greatness, like the ooze of oil
Crushed.   Why do men then now not reck his rod?
Generations have trod, have trod, have trod;
　　And all is seared with trade; bleared,
　　　　smeared with toil;
　　And wears man's smudge and shares man's smell:
　　　　the soil
Is bare now, nor can foot feel, being shod.

And for all this, nature is never spent;
　　There lives the dearest freshness deep down things;
And though the last lights off the black West went
　　Oh, morning, at the brown brink eastward,
　　　　springs -
Because the Holy Ghost over the bent
World broods with warm breast and with ah !
　　　　bright wings.

Gerard Manley Hopkins (1844 - 1889)
****

Silence gives us a new outlook on everything. We need
silence to be able to touch souls. The essential thing is not
what we say but what God says through us. Jesus is always
waiting for us in silence. In that silence, he will listen to us,
there he will speak to our souls, and there we will hear his
voice.

The world today is hungry not only for bread but hungry for
love; hungry to be wanted, to be loved. They're hungry to feel
that presence of Christ. In many countries, people have
everything except that presence, that understanding. That's
why the life of prayer and sacrifice comes to give that love.

Jesus came into the world for one purpose. He came to give
us the good news that God loves us, that God is love, that he
loves you, and he loves me. He wants us to love one another
as he loves each one of us. Let us love him.

Mother Teresa of Calcutta
"Jesus the Word to be Spoken"

Little Gidding

With the dawning of this Love
     and the voice of this Calling
We shall not cease from exploration
And the end of all our exploring
Will be to arrive where we started
And to know the place for the first time.
Through the unknown, remembered gate
When the last of earth left to discover
Is that which was the beginning;
At the source of the longest river
The voice of the hidden waterfall
And the children in the apple-tree
Not known, because not looked for
But heard, half-heard, in the stillness
Between two waves of the sea.
Quick now, here, now, always -
A condition of complete simplicity
(Costing not less than everything)
And shall be well and
And all manner of thing shall be well
When the tongues of flame are in-folded
Into the crowned knot of fire
And the fire and the rose are one.

T. S. Eliot (1888 – 1965)

The Journey of the Magi

  All this was a long time ago, I remember,
And I would do it again, but set down
This set down   This : were we led all that way for
Birth or Death?   There was Birth, certainly,
We had evidence and no doubt.
  I had seen birth and death,
But had thought they were different; this Birth was
Hard and bitter agony for us, like Death, our death.
We returned to our places, these Kingdoms,
But no longer at ease here, in the old dispensation,
With an alien people clutching their gods.
I should be glad of another death.

T. S. Eliot (1888 – 1965)

How late I came to you,
O Beauty so ancient and so fresh,
How late I came to love you!

You were within me, yet I had gone outside to seek you.
Unlovely myself,
I rushed towards all those lovely thing you had made.
And always you were within me, I was not with you.

All these beauties kept me far from you –
although they would not have existed at all
unless they had their being in you.

You called, you cried, you shattered my deafness.

You sparkled, you blazed, you drove away my blindness.

You shed your fragrance, and I drew in my breath
and I pant for you.

I tasted   and now I hunger and thirst.

You touched me,
and now I burn with longing for your peace.

The Confessions of St. Augustine   (354 – 430)

****

Take, Lord, and receive
        all my memory,
                my understanding
                        and my entire will -
                                all that I have and call my own.

You have given it all to me.
        To you, Lord, I return it.
                Everything is yours;
                        do with it what you will.

Give me only your love
        and you grace.
                That is enough for me.

Ignatius of Loyola

Trust in the slow work of God.
We are, quite naturally, impatient in everything
            to reach the end without delay.
We should like to skip the intermediate stages.
We are impatient of being on the way
            to something unknown,
            something new.

And yet it is the law of all progress
            that it is made by passing through
            some stage of instability -
            and that may take a very long time.

And so I think it is with you.
Your ideas mature gradually.
Let them grow.
Let them shape themselves without undue haste.

Don't try to force them on,
            as though you could be today
            what time - that is to say,
            grace and circumstances
            acting on your own good will -
            will make you tomorrow.

Only God could say what this new spirit
            gradually forming within you
            will be.

Give our Lord the benefit of believing
            that God's hand is leading you
            and accept the anxiety
            of feeling yourself in suspense and incomplete.

A reading from Pierre Teilhard de Chardin

Becoming the Beloved is the great spiritual journey we have to make. Augustine's words: "My soul is restless until it rests in you, O God", captures well this journey.

I know that the fact that I am always searching for God, always struggling to discover the fullness of love, always yearning for the complete truth, tells me that I have already been given a taste of God, of Love and of Truth. I can only look for something that I have, to some degree, already found.

How can I search for beauty and truth unless that beauty and truth are already known to me in the depth of my heart?

It seems that all of us human beings have deep inner memories of the paradise that we have lost. May be the word "innocence" is better than the word "paradise".

We were innocent before we started feeling guilty; we were in light before we entered into darkness; we were at home before we started to search for a home.

Deep in the recesses of our minds and hearts there lies hidden the treasure we seek. We know its precariousness, and we know that it holds the gift we most desire: a life stronger than death.

Henri J. M. Nouwen

****

The freedom of the other person includes all that we mean by a person's nature, individuality, endowment. It also includes their weaknesses and oddities, which are such a trial to our patience, everything that produces friction, conflicts and collisions among us.

To bear the burdens of the other person means involvement with the created reality of the other, to accept and affirm it, and, in bearing with it, to break through to the point where we take joy in it . ...

The service of forgiveness is rendered by one to the other daily. It occurs, without words, in the intercessions for one another. And every member of the fellowship, who does not grow weary in this ministry, can depend upon it, that this service is also being rendered to them by their brethren. He who is bearing others, knows that he himself is being borne, and only in this strength can he go on bearing.

"Life Together"
Dietrich Bonhoeffer (1906 - 1945)

Shadows

And if tonight my soul may find her peace
in sleep, and sink in good oblivion,
and in the morning wake like a new-opened flower
then I have been dipped again in God, and new-created.

And if, as weeks go round, in the dark of the moon
my spirit darkens and goes out, and soft strange gloom
pervades my movements and my thoughts and words
then I shall know that I am walking still with God,
we are close together now the moon's in shadow.

And if, as autumn deepens and darkens I feel the pain of
falling leaves, and stems that break in storms
and trouble and dissolution and distress
and then the softness of deep shadows folding, folding
around my soul and spirit, around my lips so sweet,
like a swoon, or more like the drowse of a low, sad song
singing darker than the nightingale, on, on to the solstice
and the silence of short days, the silence of the years, the
shadow,

then I shall know that my life is moving still with the dark
earth, and drenched with the deep oblivion of earth's lapse
and renewal.

And if, in the changing phases of man's life
I fall in sickness and in misery
my wrists seem broken and my heart seems dead
and strength is gone,
and my life is only the leavings of a life:

and still, among it all, snatches of lovely oblivion, and
snatches of renewal odd, wintry flowers upon the withered
stem, yet new, strange flowers such as my life has not
brought forth before, new blossoms of me -

then I must know that still
I am in the hands of the unknown God,
he is breaking me down to his own oblivion
to send me forth on a new morning, a new man.

D. H. Lawrence (1885 - 1930)

Thou art over us, Thou art one of us,
Thou who art - Also within us,

May all see Thee - in me also,
May I prepare the way for Thee.
May I thank Thee for all that shall fall to my lot,
May I also not forget the needs of others.

Keep me in Thy love
As Thou wouldst that all should be kept in mine.
May everything in this my being be directed to Thy glory
And may I never despair.
For I am under Thy hand.
And in Thee in all power and goodness.

Give me a pure heart - that I may see Thee,
A humble heart - that I may hear Thee,
A heart of love - that I may serve Thee,
A heart of faith - that I may abide in Thee.

Dag Hammarskjold (1905 - 61)

****

A Prayer for healing after a broken relationship

O my Lord - Wash me,
Wash me of this relationship;
Wash me of the pain of it,
Wash me of the hurt of it,
Wash me of the disappointment of it,
Wash me of the resentment of it,
Wash me of the attachment to it,
Wash me of the hurtful memories of it
that come back in the quietness, and in prayer time,
that come back in the silent night hours
and rend my body and very heart
with an agony of writhing tears.

I give myself into Your hands, Lord,
O wash me, as I lie still before You.
Do for me what I cannot do for myself.
Heal me, Lord ...

Under your healing touch
Hour by hour, and day by day
I shall be set free, until
The intention of my heart is pure love,
And until all my actions give Your lovely Name
The glory that can flow from a pure heart.

Morris Maddocks
"A Healing House of Prayer

****

It helps now and then to step back and take the long view.

The Kingdom is not only beyond our efforts
      it is beyond our vision.
We accomplish in our life-time only a tiny fraction of the
magnificent enterprise which is God's work.
Nothing we do is complete
      which is another way of saying that the Kingdom
      always lies beyond us.

No statement says all that should be said.
No prayer fully expresses our faith.
No confession brings perfection.
No pastoral visit brings wholeness.
No programme accomplishes the Church's mission.
No set of goals includes everything.

This is what we are about:
      we plant seeds that one day will grow;
      we water seeds already planted.
      knowing that the future hold promise.

We cannot do everything
and there is a sense of liberation in realising that,
this enables us to do something and do it very well.

We may never see the end results,
      but that is the difference between the master builder
      and the worker.
We are workers not master builders,
Ministers not Messiahs,
We are prophets of a future not our own.

A Prayer of Archbishop Oscar Romero

The Chinese Stonecutter

There was once a stonecutter, who was dissatisfied with himself and with his position in life.

One day, he passed a wealthy merchant's house, and through the open gateway, saw many fine possessions and important visitors. "How powerful that merchant must be!" thought the stonecutter. He became very envious, and wished that he could be like the merchant. Then he would no longer have to live the life of a mere stonecutter.

To his great surprise, he suddenly became the merchant, enjoying more luxuries and power than he had ever dreamed of, envied and detested by those less wealthy than himself. But soon a high official passed by, carried in a sedan chair, accompanied by attendants, and escorted by soldiers beating gongs. Everyone, no matter how wealthy, had to bow low before the procession. "How powerful that official is!" he thought. "I wish *I* could be a high official!"

Then he became the high official, carried everywhere in his embroidered sedan chair, feared and hated by the people all around, who had to bow before him as he passed. It was a hot summer day, and the official felt very uncomfortable in the sticky sedan chair. He looked up at the sun. It shone proudly in the sky, unaffected by his presence. "How powerful the sun is!" he thought. "I wish that *I* could be the sun!"

The he became the sun, shining fiercely down on everyone, scorching the fields, cursed by the farmers and labourers. But a huge black cloud moved between him and the earth, so that his light could no longer shine on everything below. "How powerful that storm cloud is!" he thought. "I wish that *I* could be a cloud!"

Then he became the cloud, flooding the fields and villages, shouted at by everyone. But soon he found that he was being pushed away by some great force, and realised that it was the wind. "How powerful it is!" he thought. "I wish that *I* could be the wind!"

Then he became the wind, blowing tiles off the roofs of houses, uprooting trees, hated and feared by all below him. But after a while, he ran up against something that would not move, no matter how forcefully he blew against it – a huge, towering stone. "How powerful that stone is!" he thought. I wish that *I* could be a stone.

Then he became the stone, more powerful than anything else on earth. But as he stood there, he heard the sound of a hammer pounding a chisel into the solid rock, and felt himself being changed. "What could be more powerful than I, the stone?" he thought. He looked down and saw far below him the figure of a stonecutter.

****

The Statue

"Then God said, "And now we will make human beings; they will be like us and resemble us." ... So God created human beings, making them to be like himself. He created them male and female, blessed them, and said, "Have many children, so that your descendents will live all over the earth and bring it under their control ..." - and it was done. God looked at everything that he had made, and he was very pleased."
Genesis 1; 26 – 31

Meditation One

You decide to commission a statue to be made of your self! You choose the best sculptor. The sculptor agrees . . . On condition that you do not see the statue until it is completed. Twelve months pass . . .The day comes when the sculptor rings you up to say that the statue is complete – But, he is going away for the weekend ...However, if you want to see the statue he will drop off the keys to his studio. Armed with the keys you set off to the studio - Open the door - And there you are!

- what are your feelings?- what is the statue made of?
- what does it look like? - how do you feel?

spend some time here

Meditation Two

You begin to talk to the statue and the statue talks back to you.

Talk about your impressions   Talk about your feelings

Talk about any questions that come to mind

                                   Let the conversation flow

Meditation Three

Now you become the statue! The sculptor takes you to the London Gallery for the opening of his exhibition. So the day comes . . . And (remember - you are now the statue) and the public flock in to see this latest creation, this new statue, this new you!

-   what are they saying about you?   - how are you feeling?

                    spend some time here

Meditation Four

Towards the end of the first day you notice in the crowd - someone you surprisingly recognise - It is The Lord! He comes over and with great interest examines the statue minutely. By now everyone else has left. Then he begins to speak to you

    - what does he say?   - how do you feel?

           - What conversation ensues?

Be thankful.

****

Bicycling with God

Opening: As I prepare myself for this time of prayer, I ask the Lord for a spirit of surrender and peaceful trust.

First Reading: John 12; 20 – 26 *the grain of wheat* Pause

Second Reading: Matthew 10 ; 39 *self-discovery*

Third Reading: At first I saw God as my observer, my judge, keeping an eye on me, tracking the things that I did wrong, so as to know whether I merited heaven or hell. He was out there sort of like the President or Prime Minister. I recognised his picture when I saw it, but I didn't really know him.

Later on when I recognised my higher powers, it seemed as though life was rather like a bike ride, but it was a tandem bike, and I noticed that God was in the back seat helping me to pedal. I don't know just when he suggested we changed places, but life has not been the same since, life with my higher power, that is God, makes life really exciting!

When I had control, I knew the way. It was rather boring and predictable. It was always the shortest distance between two points. But when he took the lead, he knew delightful long cuts, up mountains, and through rocky places and at breakneck speeds; it was all I could do to hang on! I worried and was anxious and asked, "Where are you taking me?" He laughed and didn't answer and I started to learn to trust.

I forgot my boring life and entered into the adventure. And when I'd say, "I'm scared," he'd lean back and touch my hand. He took me to people with gifts that I needed, gifts of healing, acceptance and joy. They gave me their gifts to take on my journey, our journey, God's and mine.

And we were off again. He said, give the gifts away; they're extra baggage, too much weight." So I did, to the people we met, and I found that in giving I received and still our burden was light.

I didn't trust him at first, in control of my life. I thought he'd wreck it. But he knows bike secrets, knows how to make it bend to take sharp corners, jump to clear high rocks, fly to shorten scary passages.

And I am learning to shut up and pedal in the strangest places, and I'm beginning to enjoy the view and the cool breeze on my face with my delightful constant companion, my higher power.

And when I'm sure I just can't do any more, he just smiles and says, "Pedal".

Pause

Meditation Exercise

Take some time to gently recall those areas in your life
where you are hanging onto the controls.

You'll know these areas because they are the concerns
which bring anxiety, loss of sleep, worry, etc.   Pause

What do you fear if you let go of the controls?   Pause

Can you let go, prayerfully, if you know
you are turning the controls over to God?   Pause

How can you begin to turn over the controls to God?
Take some time to explore this idea in the quiet.

****

The Advent

The events of history were controlled for my coming to this
world no less than for the coming of the Saviour.
The time had to be ripe ...
the place just right ...
the circumstances ready ...
before I could be born.

God chose the parents of his Son and endowed them with the
personality they needed for the Child that would be born.
I speak to God about the man and woman that he chose to be
my parents ...
until I see that they had to be the kind of human beings they
were if I was to become what God meant me to be.

The Christ child comes, like every other child,
to give the world a message.
I seek guidance from the Lord to express it
in a word ...
or image

Christ comes into the world to walk a certain path,
fulfil a certain destiny.
He consciously fulfilled what had been "written" for him.
As I look back I see in wonder what was "written"
and has thus far been fulfilled in my own life ...

113

and for each part of that script,
however small,
I say, "Thanks" ...
to make it holy with my gratitude.

I look with expectation and surrender at all that is to come
...

and, like the Christ, I say, "Yes. Let it be done ..."

Finally I recall the song the angels sang when Christ was
born.
They sang of the peace and joy that give God glory.

Have I ever heard the song the angels
sang when I was born?

I see with joy what has been done through me to make the
world a better place ...
and I join those angels in the song they sang to celebrate my
birth

****

Symbols for God and Oneself

1. Choose one of the objects below as your symbol for God.
    Spend a little time thinking about this symbol, praying
    about it,
    walking around it in your imagination
    and looking at it from all angles.

    What does it tell you about how you see God and your
    attitude to him?

2. Now choose a symbol for yourself spend a little time
    thinking about this symbol, praying about it,
    walking around it in your imagination
    and looking at it from all angles.

    What does it tell you about how you see yourself and
    your life at the moment?

    Explore the reasons for your choices in words or
    drawings.

bird	desert	feather	
city	stream		rock
word	sea	clay	
mountain		tree	
cloud	earth	sheep	
darkness		oil	
well	butterfly	candle	
flower		child	
sand	lion		cave
house		signpost	
wind	leaven		eagle

3. Finally, choose a symbol you think God, in his infinite love, would choose for you.

Is it different from the one you would choose for yourself?

(from an exercise by Colm Lavelle SJ)

****

Contemplating a Painting
As a Spiritual Exercise

The following questions may help you in looking at a painting as a prayer exercise

Spend one or two minutes on the earlier questions and longer on the later ones

1. Where does your eye first focus when you look at the painting? And then where does it travel?

2. How many colours do you see?

3. Would you consider it a bright painting or a dark one?

4. See the pattern of colour without focusing (if you wear glasses, it might help to take them off)

5. How many figures can you see?

6. Is there movement in the painting, or is it static?

7. Put yourself in the painting.
   Become each figure and see which one you feel most
   comfortable with.

8. Give the painting a name which is a feeling word.
   (e.g Joy, Anger, Peace, Hurt etc.)

9. Do you like the painting?
   Why - or why not?

10. As you look at the painting, what do you think has
    just happened
    - and what is going to happen?

11. Does it reflect your life in any way?

12. Stay with the painting and speak to the Lord about
    how it affects you.

****

Psalm 139

O God,

You know me inside and out,
through and through.
Everything I do,
every thought that flits through my mind,
every step I take,
every plan I make, every word I speak:
you know even before these things happen.
You know my past;
you know my future.
Your Presence covers my every move.
Your knowledge of me sometimes comforts me,
        sometimes frightens me;
but always, it is beyond my comprehension.

There is no way to escape you,
        no place to hide.
If I ascend to the heights of joy,
you are there before me.

If I am plunged into the depths of despair,
you are there to meet me.
I could fly to the other side of the world
        and find you there to lead the way.
I could walk into the darkest of nights
        only to find you there
        to lighten its dismal hours.

You were present at my very conception.
You guided the moulding of my unformed body
        within the womb of my mother.
Nothing about me, from beginning to end,
        was hidden from your eyes.

How amazingly wonderful it all is!

Make your all-knowing, everywhere-present Spirit
        continue to search out my feelings and
thoughts.
Free me from that which may hurt or destroy me
        and guide me along the paths of love and truth.

****

When God made the first Bird

When God made the first bird, he made just the one.
        The Bird!
Adam complained. " You know that bird?"
        The Bird!
"Yes", said God,   "What about it."
"Well , I think we - that is you, could have done better!"
GOD thought about it for a while and said,
"You've heard about when they recall a car", he said "well
I'm going to recall the bird!"
He recalled the bird and scrunched it up and made a new
little bird that could fly; small and brown and very fast. So
off it went.
Adam complained again.
"But it's boring. It's small and brown and really boring!"
"Oh!" said God.   So there was a second recall.

This time God started having fun. He found his paint box and got a basket of beaks and another of claws and set about making some exciting birds.

He painted the chest of a bird red and off it flew.
"What was that ?"   The robin.

The second bird he painted white and drew out its neck and made its bottom waterproof.
"What was that?"   A swan.

The third had a large painted beak and was the   puffin .

The fourth was big and strong and painted gold and that was the eagle.

God started to pack up his box of paints and beaks and claws, when suddenly in the distance there was a little dot.
It came closer and closer.
It was the last of the very plain little brown birds. It landed:
"I'm sorry, I'm so late, not too late am I?"
"I'm sorry," said God, "I've used all the paints and the claws and the beaks."
The bird looked so disappointed.
"Oh no it cannot be. I can't just be brown and boring."
So God looks in his paint box and there was just a spot of gold paint left.
"Open wide" he said, and God painted the back of his throat.
"Thank you, thank you, said the bird, now I 'm special too."
And he flew off .

And for the first time in the cool of the evening as God and Adam walked in the garden they heard: the nightingale sing.
God and Adam smiled.   It had been a good day's work.

God looked at Adam and thought,   "Now what could I do with Adam?

Beaks and claws? No, perhaps not."
"But how about painting him different colours and teaching him different languages?"

That could be very interesting!

Notes

Bibliography

p. 7   Sp. Ex. 18   *The Spiritual Exercises of St. Ignatius.*   Louis J. Puhl S.J. Pub: Loyola University Press p.7.

p.14   Sp. Ex. 15   *The Spiritual Exercises of St. Ignatius.*   Louis J. Puhl S.J. Pub: Loyola University Press p.6.

p.18   Vincent Donovan   *Christianity Rediscovered* Pub: Mary Knoll Orbis 1981

p.47/8, 98   *Rule for a New Brother* Foreword by Henri Nouwen Pub: Darton, Longman and Todd.

p.88   *The Star in My Heart* Joyce Rupp Ave Maria Press.

p.93   *Let Me rise and adore You* Sister Ruth The Oxford Book of Prayer, 1985.

p.96   *A Return to Love* Marianne Williamson Quoted by Nelson Mandela HarperCollins, 1992.

p.107   *A Healing House of Prayer* Morris Maddocks Hodder & Stoughton.